TELEWORK:
HOW TO TELECOMMUTE SUCCESSFULLY

A 5 Step Guide Designed for the Modern Teleworker

Hints, Tips & How to Stay Involved with your Employer

By: Nicole Bachelor & Don Philpott

Government Training Inc.™

Published by
Government Training Inc.™
ISBN: 978-1-937246-87-7

About the Publisher – Government Training Inc. ™

Government Training Inc. provides worldwide training, publishing and consulting to government agencies and contractors that support government in areas of business and financial management, acquisition and contracting, physical and cyber security and intelligence operations. Our management team and instructors are seasoned executives with demonstrated experience in areas of Federal, State, Local and DoD needs and mandates.

Recent books published by Government Training Inc. ™ include:
- ☐ The COTR Handbook
- ☐ Performance Based Contracting Handbook
- ☐ Cost Reimbursable Contracting
- ☐ Handbook for Managing Teleworkers
- ☐ Handbook for Managing Teleworkers: Toolkit
- ☐ Small Business Guide to Government Contracting
- ☐ Securing Our Schools
- ☐ Workplace Violence
- ☐ The Grant Writer's Handbook
- ☐ The Integrated Physical Security Handbook

For more information on the company, its publications and professional training, go to www.GovernmentTrainingInc.com.

Copyright © 2011 Government Training Inc. All rights reserved.

Printed in the United States of America.

This publication is protected by copyright, and permission must be obtained from the publisher prior to any prohibited reproduction, storage in a retrieval system or transmission in any form or by any means, electronic, mechanical, photocopying, recording or likewise.

For information regarding permissions, write to:
Government Training Inc. ™
Rights and Contracts Department
5372 Sandhamn Place
Longboat Key, Florida 34228
don.dickson@GovernmentTrainingInc.com

ISBN: 978-1-937246-87-7

www.GovernmentTrainingInc.com

Sources:

This book has drawn heavily on the authoritative materials published by a wide range of sources.

These materials are in the public domain, but accreditation has been given both in the text and in the reference section if you need additional information.

The author and publisher have taken great care in the preparation of this handbook, but make no expressed or implied warranty of any kind and assume no responsibility for errors or omissions.

No liability is assumed for incidental or consequential damages in connection with or arising out of the use of the information or recommendations contained herein.

Government Training Inc.™

Security Guides and Handbooks - Grants

For more information on the company, its publications and professional training, go to http://www.governmenttraininginc.com/index.asp#Bookstore.

CARVER + Shock Vulnerability Assessment Tool
A Six Step Approach to Conducting Security Vulnerability Assessments on Critical Infrastructure

CARVER has served as the standard for security vulnerability assessments for many years but it has now morphed into an even more useful tool that can be used to help protect almost any critical infrastructure.

This new no-nonsense handbook provides the security professional with background on CARVER, one of its very successful morphs into CARVER + Shock and then demonstrates how these methodologies can be applied and adapted to meet today's specific needs to protect both hard and soft targets.

The Integrated Physical Security Handbook
Securing the Nation One Facility at a Time

The Integrated Physical Security Handbook has become the recognized manual for commercial and government building and facility security managers responsible for developing security plans based on estimated risks and threats—natural or terrorist.

The Integrated Physical Security Handbook II, 2nd Edition
5-Step Process to Assess and Secure Critical Infrastructure From All Hazards Threats

This new edition covers a number of additional areas including convergence of systems, building modeling, emergency procedures, privacy issues, cloud computing, shelters and safe areas and disaster planning. There is also a comprehensive glossary as well as access to a dedicated website at www.physicalsecurityhandbook.com that provides purchasers of the book an on-line library of over 300 pages of additional reference materials.

Security Guides and Handbooks - Grants, continued

For more information on the company, its publications and professional training, go to
http://www.governmenttraininginc.com/index.asp#Bookstore.

School Security
A Physical Security Handbook for School Security Managers
The School Security Handbook provides an easy to follow, easy to implement five step process for developing an emergency response plan that covers almost any eventuality. It covers the four phases of an emergency: mitigation and prevention, preparedness, response and recovery.

Workplace Violence
A Seven-Step Process To Address and Manage Potentially Violent Situations in the WorkplaceCovering the Full Life-cycle of the Event from Prevention—Awareness—Mitigation—Response
The book is packed with useful tips, best practices, case studies and checklists that walk you through the process from understanding the violence cycle to implementing an effective WVP program and ensuring that all management and employees are aware of it.

Grant Writer's Handbook
A 5-Step Process & Toolkit to Achieve State & Local Grant Success Goals
The easy to follow Five Step process leads you through the tortuous world of grant writing – starting with how to select the right grant writer and then following the process from where to find grants in the first place to writing winning grant submissions.

Government Training Inc.™

Business Management

For more information on the company, its publications and professional training, go to http://www.governmenttraininginc.com/index.asp#Bookstore.

Handbook for Managing Teleworkers
A 5-Step Management Process for Managing Teleworkers

This book is an A-Z guide aimed at managers tasked with introducing teleworking or overseeing teleworkers and ensuring that everything runs smoothly. The rules for managing teleworking are the same whether you are a federal or state employee or work for a private company or organization. The book is also very useful to people who are thinking of teleworking or trying to persuade their employers to introduce it.

Handbook for Managing Teleworkers – Toolkit

The Handbook discusses all the arguments that have been put forward against teleworking and debunks them using all the latest surveys and case studies. There are chapters on problems and how to overcome them and how to motivate through counseling, coaching and developing trust.

It is an invaluable resource for all telework managers and those who might be tasked with taking on this responsibility and an essential companion guide to Government Institute's Handbook for Managing Teleworkers published earlier this year.

Executive Briefings & Presentations Best Practices Handbook
A step by step process and guide to making powerful presentations to colleagues and the press

This book will teach how you to develop a plan so that you know what to do, what to say and how best to say it. These techniques will stand you in good stead whenever you need to communicate whether it is in the office or in front of millions of people during a live television interview.

Government Training Inc.™

Business Management, continued

For more information on the company, its publications and professional training, go to http://www.governmenttraininginc.com/index.asp#Bookstore.

How To Get Others To Do What You Want Them To Do
(Or... Never Kick a Kangaroo!)

Wouldn't it be great if you always got your way in negotiations and never lost another argument? We all have the tools to achieve this but most of us don't know how to use them. That is what Never Kick a Kangaroo is all about. It may be a strange title but you would never get into a kick boxing fight with a kangaroo – you would lose. In order to be successful you must understood the other participants – what they want and the tools they use. You can then pick the tools and techniques that will work in your favor.

GovCloud: Cloud Computing for the Business of Government
A Five-Step Process to Evaluate, Design and Implement a Robust Cloud Solution

The book describes the key characteristics of cloud computing and various deployment and delivery models. It contains case studies and best practices, how to set and meet goals, developing a robust business case analysis, how to implement and use cloud computing and how to make sure it is working.

Government Training Inc.™

Contracting and Acquisition

For more information on the company, its publications and professional training, go to http://www.governmenttraininginc.com/index.asp#Bookstore.

The COTR Handbook
A Five-Step Process for Stronger Organizational Performance

This handbook looks at the complex duties performed by COTRs and explains how best to carry them out in order to achieve a stronger organizational performance. The easy-to-follow Five Step Process explains the environment in which the COTR operates, how the COTR and other team players are selected, key skill areas required and how these are applied throughout the contracting process. Finally, we discuss how the COTR's influence can be extended through developing a career model, continuous training and extending this to broader applications across other organizational activities.

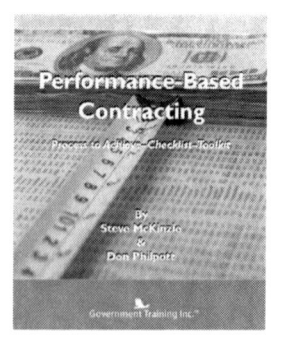

Performance-Based Contracting
Process to Achieve–Checklist–Toolkit

The book shows you how to write a successful performance-based statement of work with lots of case studies and examples. Chapters lead you through all the steps necessary – from planning and market research to writing the performance-based statement of work and everything in between.

Managing Cost Reimbursable Contracts
Providing Guidance in Difficult Waters

The Handbook is packed with practical information, handy hints, real-life case studies, best practices and checklists. It describes the different types of cost-reimbursable contracts, when they should be used and why, and when they are not the appropriate contracting vehicle. It also details the dangers inherent in this type of contract and how they can be recognized and controlled.

Government Training Inc.™

Contracting and Acquisition, continued

For more information on the company, its publications and professional training, go to http://www.governmenttraininginc.com/index.asp#Bookstore.

Guide to Independent Government Cost Estimating (IGCE)
Five Step Process Leading to Best Practice Estimates

The Guide provides an expanded overview of the federal acquisition process and the role played by independent government cost estimates. The information is accented by well-grounded discussion of the statutory and regulatory basis for cost estimates. The Guide then introduces a five-step process leading to best practice estimates. The five steps are presented with clarity and designed to be quickly understood and applied.

The Federal Acquisition Regulation (FAR)
Two Book Set: Desk Reference
For Government and Corporate Acquisition and Contracting staff

Includes all updates through January 12, 2011

2 Book Set: Desk Reference

This two volume set is designed for ease of use and transport. Both volumes (Volume 1 and 2) include a full Table of Contents and reference matrix to facilitate look-ups and research. Paper choice was selected to allow marking and highlighting without serious bleed-through – an important ease of use feature.

Small Business Guide to Government Contracting
A Guide to Small Businesses Entering Government Contracting

If you have never done business with the federal government before, the manual leads you through an easy to understand five-step process of what to do and how to do it in order to maximize your chances for a successful contract bid. If you already do business with the Federal government, the manual is packed with tips and hints, best practices and case studies to help you improve your outcomes.

Contents

Introduction 1

Step 1. Is Telecommuting Right for Me? 3
   Advantages of Telecommuting 3
   Potential Downsides of Telecommuting 4
   Tasks Suitable for Telework 5
   Am I Suited to Telecommuting? 6

Step 2. How do I get a job Telecommuting? 15
   Convincing Your Boss 15
   My job Just Isn't Suited to Telecommuting 22
   You are Unemployed 23
   Who's Hiring 24
   The Private Sector V Federal Sector 26

Step 3. Combining Work and Family 29
   Childcare 29
   Why Bother? 31
      Working with Dependents and Disabilities 32

Step 4. The Home Office 39
   Your 'Office' 39
   Ergonomics 40
   Hardware and Connectivity 42

Step 5: Working at Home 47
   Out-of-sight, Out-of-mind 47
   Communication Styles 49
   Improving Your Virtual Presence 50
   The Phone 51
      One-on-One Phone Meetings 51
      Phone Meetings With Your Manager 53
      Keeping the Attention During Phone Calls 54
   Email 56
      The Single Most Important Lesson When Using Email 56
      Make Your Message Clear 58
      Message Recipients 61
      Email Etiquette 66

Telework: How to Telecommute Successfully

Reporting Status 69
Instant Messaging 70
   Which IM Tool to Use 71
   Using IM Well 71
   IM Mistakes 73
   Communicating Differently 75
   IM Summary 76
Group Meetings and Collaboration Tools 77
   Collaboration Tools 77
   Running a Group Meeting 78
You are the Only Virtual Attendee 84
Isolation 87
   Professional Networking 90
   Consider a Mentor 92
   Co-Worker Hostility 93
Discipline 94
   Avoiding Distractions at Home 94
   Work-Life Balance 97
Conclusion 99

Appendix **101**
Appendix 1. Countering Management Doubts and Concerns 101
Appendix 2. Teleworking and IT Security 104
Appendix 3. Remote Access Methods 114
Appendix 4. Legal Rights of Teleworkers 119
Appendix 5. Safety and Working from Home 120
Appendix 6. Samples of Teleworking Policies 131
   Example 1 131
   Example 2. Sample Telework Suitability Worksheet 136
   Example 3. Sample Telework Agreement – Oregon Office of Energy 138
   Example 4. Sample Corporate Telework Policy and Agreement 146
   Example 5. Telework Policy Template 147

About the authors

Nicole Bachelor

Nicole Bachelor is a professional, experienced telecommuter and has lectured and taught extensively on this subject. Her upbeat, positive style communicates her balanced approach to creating a win-win for telecommuter and manager. Her focus includes the development of management process and tools that enable successful telecommuting.

She has been telecommuting exclusively for over 4 years, and working from home at least a few days per week for many years before that. Nicole, who works at a large, high-tech company based in Silicon Valley, was able to rise to top ranking in her job while telecommuting full-time.

Nicole was the author and key presenter of a national webinar series on How to Manage Telecommuters produced by Government Training Inc. The webinar that was set up to address the new federal government telecommuting initiative based on the Federal Telecommuting Improvement Act passed by conference in the winter of 2010.

Don Philpott

Don Philpott is editor of International Homeland Security, a quarterly journal for homeland security professionals, and has been writing, reporting and broadcasting on international events, trouble spots and major news stories for more than 40 years. For 20 years he was a senior correspondent with Press Association -Reuters, the wire service, and traveled the world on assignments including Northern Ireland, Lebanon, Israel, South Africa and Asia.

He writes for magazines and newspapers in the United States and Europe and is a contributor to radio and television programs on security and other issues. He is the author of more than 90 books on a wide range of subjects and has had more than 5,000 articles printed in publications around the world. His most recent books are Handbook for COTRs, Performance Based Contracting, Cost Reimbursable Contracting, How to Manage Teleworkers and just released, How to Manage Teleworkers: Toolkit. All of these books have been published by Government Training Inc.

He is a member of the National Press Club.

Symbols

Throughout this book you will see a number of icons displayed in the margins. The icons are there to help you as you work through the Five Step process. Each icon acts as an advisory – for instance alerting you to things that you must always do or should never do. The icons used are:

Must Do — This is something that you must always do

No No — This is something you should never do

Tips — Really useful tips

Remember — Points to bear in mind

Checklist — Have you checked off or answered everything on this list?

Introduction

I have probably written the majority of this book while wearing my pajamas. For that matter, I have probably performed the majority of my job, for the last four years or more, in my pajamas.

Here's what a typical day looks like for me:

6:30 am – Roll out of bed and sit right down in front of the computer. Start looking through my inbox to see if any emergencies cropped up while I was asleep or if there are any urgent emails I have to respond to – especially from my European coworkers. Maybe take a phone meeting.

7:30 am – Get the kids up, fed, and dressed so when the nanny arrives she can take my son to pre-school.

8:30 am – Pour myself a bowl of cereal and hop right back onto my computer. I probably have back-to-back phone meetings now for the next few hours – group meetings that include my European counterparts.

12:30 pm – Notice the time. Notice my stomach growling. Drag myself away from my computer and go make some lunch. Take a break to chat with my nanny and play with my baby daughter. If I've been organized enough the night before to prep dinner, I turn on the crock-pot and let food start to cook. Take my lunch back to my computer and get back to work.

2:30 pm – Notice the time. Go take a shower and get out of my pajamas! Take another little break to cuddle with my baby daughter. Return to work and hop on the emails from my Australian coworkers so I can get a few back-and-forth conversations with them by email before the end of my day.

5:00 pm – Stop work. Poke at the food in the crock-pot. Let the nanny head home. Pickup my son from preschool, greet my husband when he gets home (and be thankful I got around to the shower today) and start the evening chaos with two small children, dinner, bath times, bedtimes, etc.

8:15 pm – Done getting the kids to bed. Return to my computer for 10 minutes to see if any urgent emails have come in from my Asian coworkers. Or if my boss (two time zones ahead of me) has been working in the evening, I can send a quick reply to him so he can have his answers when he first gets up in the morning (plus it looks like I'm working hard when he sees emails sent from me at 8:30 pm!).

8:30 pm – Sit down to rest in front of the TV for an hour or two before I crawl into bed, pass out, and repeat the next day!

Some people might find this blending and melding of personal life and work an ideal, dream work situation. Others might be appalled. I will not lie to you and tell you that full-time telecommuting is right for everyone. However, for many people it gives huge advantages and for just about everyone, occasional telecommuting can really simplify life.

Nicole Bachelor

Note: Don Philpott has teleworked for the last 20 years – but not in his PJs!

This book will help you figure out if telecommuting is right for you, how to convince your boss to let you do it, and, most importantly, how to do it successfully.

Step 1. Is Telecommuting Right for Me?

In general, the occasional day spent working from home (because you're expecting the plumber/cable guy/ important delivery or because you have a mid-day checkup with the dentist) is a common theme. But what about more serious telecommuting — either daily, or consistently for a few days per week?

Advantages of Telecommuting

Well first, let's examine the advantages. Although some may be obvious to you, you may not have considered them all. And these, stacked up against any disadvantages or concerns you may have, are worth considering.

- ☐ Roll out of bed and work in your pajamas!
- ☐ Eliminate your commute time (and spend the spare time as you choose).
- ☐ Avoid the cost of commuting.
- ☐ Avoid the frustration and road rage from fighting traffic during your commute.
- ☐ Improve the quality of the environment by taking one more car off the road.
- ☐ Reduce interruptions from co-workers and office buddies when you really need to focus and get things done.
- ☐ Save money by grabbing meals from the fridge instead of paying the over-priced cafeteria costs for lousy, less-than-healthy meals.
- ☐ Save time:
  - For yourself — you can be there to have breakfast with your children or make it to that soccer practice once in a while, or squeeze in your doctor or dentist appointment.
  - For your job — it's much easier to take early morning or late evening phone calls with coworkers in other parts of the world.
- ☐ Save money by not having to buy expensive office clothes (and not having to send them to the dry cleaners).

Potential Downsides of Telecommuting

Remember: The list in the previous section looks pretty good huh? However, there are some potential downsides to telecommuting. You should not consider these as show-stoppers. This book will arm you with the knowledge to deal with these and more, and, in some cases, to use them to your advantage!

- ☐ Less face time with your boss and coworkers – out of sight can mean out of mind.
- ☐ Taking meetings by phone means you lose the information transmitted by eye contact, facial expression, and body language that you would get in a face-to-face meeting.
- ☐ More challenging to learn and receive guidance from co-workers or your boss.
- ☐ Fewer chances to directly oversee subordinates.
- ☐ Sense of isolation working alone in your home.
- ☐ Potential distractions in your house (the fridge calling you, the dirty laundry calling you, the fridge calling you, urges to tidy up around the house, the fridge calling you, an unexpected visit from the neighbor, did I mention the fridge calling you?).
- ☐ Interruptions from friends and family who don't understand that "working from home" still means "working."
- ☐ Working too much (yes, you read that right) – not being able to stop at the end of the work day.
- ☐ Losing your downtime opportunity on your way to and from work (assuming your commute isn't too frustrating and you enjoy a little time to think in the car or read on the train).

Now, we didn't write this list to frighten you. Knowing the potential pitfalls is half the battle. Most people simply fail to consider or acknowledge that there's anything to be careful of and that's why they struggle. But we know you're not going into this with your eyes closed – after all, you were concerned enough to buy this book!

The first two bullets relate to the lack of direct face-to-face interaction with your boss and co-workers. There are a number of techniques we'll discuss on how to deal with this.

The rest of the bullets can all be answered with some simple techniques we will discuss and just a little bit of discipline to stick to those techniques.

Telework is NOT:
- Work extension: many employees take work home with them. This is remote work, but it is not considered to be telework within the scope of the legislation.

Step 1. Is Telecommuting Right for Me?

- Mobile work: some agencies have employees who, by the nature of their jobs, are generally offsite, and may even have their homes as "home base." Since the nature of their work requires this setup – usually, they are traveling much of the time – they are not considered to be teleworkers. This is different from "hoteling" arrangements, in which frequent teleworkers share space when onsite.
- An employee right: federal law requires agencies to have telework programs, but does not give individual employees a legal right to telework.

Tasks Suitable for Telework

Telework can accommodate a wide range of tasks. Common examples include, but are not limited to:

- ☐ Independent Thinking and Writing
    - Researching a topic
    - Analyzing data
    - Reviewing proposals or contracts
    - Responding to correspondence
    - Drafting reports or other documents
- ☐ Telephone Use
    - Setting up a conference
    - Obtaining information
    - Following up with customers
- ☐ Computer Use
    - Programming
    - Graphic design
    - Web page design
    - Data entry
    - Word processing
    - Desktop publishing

The following is a sample of professions and job duties that typically can be considered for teleworking:

Accountant	Administrative Assistant	Agent	Appraiser
Architect	Auditor	Budget Analyst	Computer Scientist
Consultant	Contract Monitor	Customer	Data Analysis
Data Entry Clerk	Economist	Employment Interviewer	Engineer
Financial Analyst	Investigator	Journalist	Lawyer

Manager	Payroll transaction processing	Programmer	Psychologist
Scientist	Service Researcher	Systems Analyst	Tax Examiner
Telephone-intensive tasks	Training Designer	Transcriptionist	Web page design
Word processing	Writer		

While many tasks are suitable for telework, some tasks require the employee's physical presence in the office. Unsuitable tasks may include those that involve:

- ☐ Extensive face-to-face contact with the manager, coworkers, or other agency staff, although be careful what you consider as necessary face-to-face contact – you'll be surprised how much can be achieved without the face-to-face contact once you get the telecommuting skills down!
- ☐ Access to systems, equipment, or material that cannot be moved from the office.
- ☐ Safeguards and control due to security requirements.

Remember: The ideal situation is to divide up the workweek so the telework-suitable tasks that can be done from a remote location, with the remainder being accomplished in the office. With that in mind, the exact number of telework days depends on four factors:

- ☐ The manager's comfort level with how many teleworkers can be out of the office for how many days a week.
- ☐ The teleworker's comfort level with the number of days he/she is willing to work remotely.
- ☐ The needs of coworkers and clients.
- ☐ Any limitations on office space availability in the central office and/or at a telework center.

Am I Suited to Telecommuting?

So now you know the advantages and disadvantages of telecommuting, and which types of roles/tasks are suited to telecommuting, the next question to ask is whether you are suited to telecommuting. While most people are quite well-suited to telecommuting at least part of the time, there are a few people who may not be.

And of course, how well-suited you are, is in part determined by how badly you want to telecommute. You can make just about anything work well if you are sufficiently motivated!

Step 1. Is Telecommuting Right for Me?

Answer the following questions honestly:

- Do you find you can get more done on a day when there are fewer people around, and if you could just have a few hours of uninterrupted time, you could plow through that report that your boss has been nagging you about?
- Do you hate commuting?
- Are you able to successfully collaborate on work activities by phone with one or two people?
- Do you enjoy peace and quiet when you are working?
- Do you want to have more time available for your family?
- Do you want to have more control over your working hours?
- Can you stay sufficiently self-motivated to manage your own daily schedule (e.g. avoid the temptation to sleep until noon)?
- Do you have a little discipline when it comes to avoiding distractions?
- If you have young children, do you have childcare arranged?
- Are you able to find energy from within (rather than needing to be around a big group of people to be energized)?

If you answered yes to at least some of these questions, then read on!

Even if you answered no to almost every question, please keep reading. Perhaps there's information in this book that will help turn enough of those no's into yes's and allow you to make some regularly scheduled telecommuting fit into your lifestyle and work style.

What distinguishes a good teleworker? For starters, he/she typically:

- Is able to work with minimal direct supervision
- Has been in the job and department long enough to be able to solve many of his/her own problems and answer many of his/her own questions
- Has demonstrated the ability to "deliver the goods" on time and according to specifications, and has effective time-management skills
- Has demonstrated the ability to initiate and guide his/her own work and is the proverbial "self-starter" who does not need to be reminded to get the job done
- Can and does communicate effectively with a variety of others, using a mix of personal and electronic means as is appropriate

Employee Assessment Questionnaire

The following questionnaire can be used as a guide for evaluating an employee's potential for successful telework. Rather than being a performance review or rating, it is an evaluation of individual work characteristics, habits, and competencies and an indicator of the likelihood of an employee's success.

Think through these questions carefully and answer them as fairly and objectively as possible.

The following is the sort of questionnaire you might be asked to answer by an employer. Before you fill it in, it is a good idea to discuss it with your employer to ensure you are both on the same page. Copies will likely be put in your file, and it is a good idea to repeat this exercise at least every year or when your working circumstances change significantly.

Employee Assessment Questionnaire

Employee Name:			
Employee Position:			
1. Provide a brief summary of employee's duties and responsibilities.			
2. Evaluate the following work characteristics according to the employee's existing job function (place a check under the appropriate column)			
	LOW	MEDIUM	HIGH
Clarity of goals and objectives for the position			
Ability to schedule face-to-face contact (meetings, etc.) on certain days of the week			
Degree to which communications can be accomplished using voice mail, email, faxing, electronic file transfer			
Ability to control work flow or schedule			
Reliability of technology to support employee when teleworking			
3. Evaluate the following work characteristics according to the employee's existing job function (place a check under the appropriate column).			
	LOW	MEDIUM	HIGH
Amount of in-office face-to-face contact required			
Amount of in-office reference materials or other resources required			
Impact on work team when employee is teleworking			
4. Evaluate the employee's work style and level of performance characteristics (place a check under the appropriate column).			
	LOW	MEDIUM	HIGH
Level of job knowledge			
Experience on current assignment			
Level of organizing and planning skills			
Need for supervisor and/or frequent feedback			
Self-discipline regarding work			

Telework: How to Telecommute Successfully

that you work for. At the end of the three profiles is a summary that provides an overview of the responses given.

Section 1: Job Requirements Profile				
Tasks and Functions are Distinct or Readily Defined				
☐ Always	☐ Most of the Time	☐ About Half the Time	☐ Rarely	☐ Never
Work can be Scheduled or Time Controlled				
☐ Always	☐ Most of the Time	☐ About Half the Time	☐ Rarely	☐ Never
Quantity and Quality of Work are Measurable				
☐ Always	☐ Most of the Time	☐ About Half the Time	☐ Rarely	☐ Never
Quality of Worker's Performance can Remain High				
☐ Always	☐ Most of the Time	☐ About Half the Time	☐ Rarely	☐ Never
Quality of Colleagues' Performance can Remain High				
☐ Always	☐ Most of the Time	☐ About Half the Time	☐ Rarely	☐ Never
Quality of Customer Service can Remain High				
☐ Always	☐ Most of the Time	☐ About Half the Time	☐ Rarely	☐ Never
Can be Performed Without Special Equipment				
☐ Always	☐ Most of the Time	☐ About Half the Time	☐ Rarely	☐ Never
Can be Performed by Other Staff on a Back-up Basis				
☐ Always	☐ Most of the Time	☐ About Half the Time	☐ Rarely	☐ Never
Section 2: Employee Success Profile				
Performs at or Above Expected Levels				
☐ Always	☐ Most of the Time	☐ About Half the Time	☐ Rarely	☐ Never
Understands Job Responsibilities				
☐ Always	☐ Most of the Time	☐ About Half the Time	☐ Rarely	☐ Never
Works Well Independently				
☐ Always	☐ Most of the Time	☐ About Half the Time	☐ Rarely	☐ Never
Reliable and Accountable				
☐ Always	☐ Most of the Time	☐ About Half the Time	☐ Rarely	☐ Never
Communicates Well				
☐ Always	☐ Most of the Time	☐ About Half the Time	☐ Rarely	☐ Never
Maintains Good Relationships with Peers and Customers				
☐ Always	☐ Most of the Time	☐ About Half the Time	☐ Rarely	☐ Never
Organizes Work Well, Including Multiple Assignments				
☐ Always	☐ Most of the Time	☐ About Half the Time	☐ Rarely	☐ Never

Step 1. Is Telecommuting Right for Me?

Flexible				
☐ Always	☐ Most of the Time	☐ About Half the Time	☐ Rarely	☐ Never
Section 3: Management Profile				
Manages by Objectives and Results				
☐ Always	☐ Most of the Time	☐ About Half the Time	☐ Rarely	☐ Never
Comfortable Managing Nontraditional Work Situations				
☐ Always	☐ Most of the Time	☐ About Half the Time	☐ Rarely	☐ Never
Flexible				
☐ Always	☐ Most of the Time	☐ About Half the Time	☐ Rarely	☐ Never
Communicates Well				
☐ Always	☐ Most of the Time	☐ About Half the Time	☐ Rarely	☐ Never
Provides Coaching				
☐ Always	☐ Most of the Time	☐ About Half the Time	☐ Rarely	☐ Never
Able To Trust Subordinates				
☐ Always	☐ Most of the Time	☐ About Half the Time	☐ Rarely	☐ Never
Promotes Empowerment				
☐ Always	☐ Most of the Time	☐ About Half the Time	☐ Rarely	☐ Never
Open to New Ideas				
☐ Always	☐ Most of the Time	☐ About Half the Time	☐ Rarely	☐ Never

Part 1: Job Requirements

Tasks and Functions are Distinct and Readily Defined
Do tasks have clear beginning and end points?

Work can be Scheduled or Time Controlled
Can work be assigned for particular days of the week? Can work be accomplished within a set time frame with clear deadlines?

Quantity and Quality of Work are Measurable
Can you track the amount of work produced? Can you easily assess the quality of the work performed?

Quality of Worker's Performance can Remain High
Will the proposed job arrangement enable the worker to perform as well or better than he/she does now?

Step 1. Is Telecommuting Right for Me?

Maintains Good Relationships with Peers and Customers

Does your employee have good relationships with peers, customers, and team members? Will he/she be able to accomplish team assignments and inter-agency projects?

Organizes Work Well, Including Multiple Assignments

Is your employee well organized? Is he/she able to set priorities and accomplish work efficiently? Is he/she able to work on several assignments simultaneously?

Flexible

Is your employee flexible? Has he/she been willing to take on new assignments? Is he/she willing to switch scheduled workdays if necessary or adjust his/her work schedule?

Part 3: Management Profile

Manages by Objectives and Results

Do you provide employees with clear direction on the tasks to be performed and the results you expect?

Comfortable Managing Nontraditional Work Situations

Do you keep your employees informed about the status of assignments, projects, and work issues? Do you clearly and consistently communicate your expectations of employee performance? Do you give clear and consistent feedback to employees on their performance?

Flexible

Are you able to be flexible in the face of changing circumstances or work arrangements?

Communicates Well

Do you keep your employees informed about the status of assignments, projects, and work issues? Do you clearly and consistently communicate your expectations of employee performance? Do you give clear and consistent feedback to employees on their performance?

Provides Coaching

Do you assist employees in building their skills and competencies? Do you coach them on areas they need to improve upon and/or provide them with training opportunities?

Able To Trust Subordinates

Do you believe that employees in nontraditional work situations will be responsible in the performance of their duties?

Promotes Empowerment

Are you able to give your employees the freedom to work on their own and/or to manage their own work schedules? Do you believe that opportunities to use nontraditional work situations will contribute to your employees' growth and development?

Open to New Ideas

Are you open to considering different ways to get a job done as long as it is successfully completed?

Step 2. How do I get a job Telecommuting?

So, you want to telecommute and, armed with the information you'll read in the rest of this book, you know you can do it successfully.

But now what?

If you're really lucky, your company is already very supportive of telecommuting and all you need to do is casually mention to your boss that you want to start working from home, and you're ready to go.

Good for you. Sign up for telecommuting and skip the rest of this chapter!

However, many of you will not find yourself so fortunate. Quite possibly you're in one of three circumstances:

1. You work for a company that doesn't have an active, supportive policy towards telecommuting, but if you make the effort you can probably convince your boss to let you give it a try.
2. You're in the type of job where telecommuting really isn't possible.
3. You're unemployed.

Convincing Your Boss

Let's start with the first situation. You're at a company that doesn't actively encourage telecommuting, but you know of a couple of folks who do it and you think you can probably convince your boss. Even if you're not sure if you can convince him/her, it's worth a shot and you feel you have little to lose.

The key here is to be prepared before approaching your boss on this topic. Don't just wander into his/her office and ask if you can telecommute.

Must Do

If your boss has a lot on his plate and is working long hours and dealing with difficult politics from above, the last thing he'll want to do is start adding complications with his staff. It's much easier for him to say no than take a risk.

The first thing you want to do is convince your boss that this is not just an annoyance at best and a significant disruption at worst. You actually want him to understand that this is an advantage for him and for the company overall. Let's look at some reasons it's in your company's best interest to let you telecommute:

Advantages for a company to let their employees telecommute:

☐ Enhancement to employee perks –
- Telecommuting is a clear advantage for many employees; one that can increase those people's enjoyment of the job and assist with work-life balance.
- A company that provides this option to their employees is showing that it respects and values its human resources. For the same salaries, such a company can attract better talent, and increase the loyalty and long-term commitment of its existing employees.

☐ Significant retention factor for some employees –
- Some employees consider the ability to telecommute (due to a very significant commute, or family demands) a critical factor in their job.
- Some people will leave a company altogether if they can't telecommute – and these are normally the top employees who can easily get a new job with the same pay and a telecommuting option somewhere else.
- These top employees provide a significant value to their company and are a major loss when they leave. Additionally the costs to hire and train a new employee to replace the old one are very significant to a company – this is something they want to avoid wherever possible.

☐ Cost savings in real-estate, physical infrastructure, and operations –
- The costs of office space for a company are significant.
- Each employee takes up a cubicle or office – and that space has to be paid for. If full-time telecommuters give up their office, or part-time telecommuters agree to share an office, office space can be consolidated (or new offices don't need to be bought as the company grows).
- This may not seem like much to you but it adds up, and in some parts of the world real-estate is at a premium!
- But it's not just the real-estate costs. Think about the other costs in an office building – electricity to run all those computers, network and phone lines, printers, faxes, desk-side support, cleaning, maintenance, insurance.

The list adds up quickly.

In a perfect world, you'll convince your company to help share some of the costs of your home Internet access and second phone line, but you may have to foot the bill on this one.

Step 2. How do I get a job Telecommuting?

Tip: See the cost-saving tips in Chapter 4 to be able to afford to get your manager to agree.

- ☐ Increased productivity from employees –
  - As already discussed, working from home often means less interruptions from co-worker gossip, etc., so you can buckle down and get your work done. This is good for your manager and your company!
  - Additionally, what about all the commuting time that is saved? Sure, some of it you'll take back for your own personal time, but people who telecommute do tend to work slightly longer hours – probably because they can do this and still have time left over for themselves.
- ☐ Increased availability and flexibility from employees –
  - If you're all set up to work from home, then it's easier to do just that – work from home any time you need to. Occasionally there might be an early morning or late evening meeting that you need to attend. Or simply your boss has an urgent question for you at the end of the day.
  - For many non-telecommuters, their computer stays at the office, and when they go home for the day they're out of reach.
  - But your boss knows that if your computer is all set up and running at home, there's at least a chance you'll be glancing at emails in the evening, or willing to dive into work during non-standard hours once in a while for a special urgent need.
- ☐ Environmentally Conscious
  - Obviously the absence of a commute (assuming you drive) is an advantage for the environment. We all know about the damage being done by the huge number of cars on the road today.
  - Most companies care a lot about their corporate image and make efforts to be involved in programs that are socially responsible. Allowing their employees to telecommute shows the public that this company cares about the environment and is making an effort to help.

So when you approach your boss on this subject, don't go in feeling that you're asking for something that's all for you, with a hang-dog, apologetic, please-don't-be-mad-at-me-for-asking-this attitude. Instead, tell him you want to telecommute and sit down and talk to him first about the advantages, from his perspective, of letting you.

Make him want you to telecommute. Make him look like a hero for supporting telecommuting. He's helping the company! Approach him with a positive, enthusiastic this-is-an-advantage-for-both-of-us attitude.

www.GovernmentTrainingInc.com

Identifying Teleworking Benefits

Remember While many private and public employers initially created teleworking programs to address environmental mandates or enhance employee work/life balance, employers currently recognize many other benefits of allowing and enabling employees to telecommute. Teleworking has the potential to provide significant benefits for employers, employees and the community.

Teleworking will help your organization in the following ways:

Productivity
- More Work Accomplished
    - Greater Focus
    - Fewer Distractions
- Job Satisfaction
    - Improved Morale
    - Greater Commitment/Loyalty
- Greater Efficiency
    - Commute Time Savings
    - Less Stress
    - Flexible Work Schedule

Cost Efficiency
- Reduces Hiring and Replacement Costs
    - Relocation Costs Hiring Expenses
    - Training Time and Expense
- Reduced Unscheduled Absences
    - Less Downtime
    - Reduced Costs Associated with Unscheduled Absences
- Real Estate Savings
    - Reduced Office Space
    - Increased Parking Efficiency
    - Shared Work Space
    - Reduced Operating Expenses
    - Controlled Expansion Expenses

Flexibility
- Less Downtime
    - Ability to Work on Snow Days
    - Ability to Work During Sick Leave

Step 2. How do I get a job Telecommuting?

- ◇ Ability to Work Remotely
- ◇ Ability to Return to Work for Injured Employees
- ☐ Retention and Attraction
  - ◇ Retention of Key Employees
  - ◇ Retention of Employees Relocating
  - ◇ Attraction of Employees Seeking Flexible Arrangement
- ☐ Wider Labor Pool
  - ◇ Access to Workers in Larger Geographic Area
  - ◇ Attract and Retain Qualified Persons with Physical Disabilities
- ☐ Less Absenteeism
  - ◇ Ability to Work Without Infecting Others With Colds, Flu, and other Contagious Illnesses
  - ◇ Ability to Work Outside of Traditional Office Hours

Teleworking will help the community:
- ☐ Decrease Traffic Congestion
- ☐ Conserve Resources Through Reduced Gasoline Consumption
- ☐ Reduce Air Pollution
- ☐ Offer More Employment Opportunities for Untapped Labor Force (e.g., disabled, part-time, retired, work-time availability)

Be prepared with a plan:

Now your boss sees there are some significant advantages to letting you telecommute, but he's still concerned that it's going to be complicated and messy, and he's worried that he may later regret a decision to allow you to do this.

☐ First, help your boss feel more comfortable by assuring him that he doesn't have to commit right away.

> **Propose a trial period.** Maybe you try telecommuting for three to six months during which he can evaluate your performance and compare it to past work.
>
> *Tips*

Or what about providing a survey to the people you work closely with at the end of the trial period and see if they still feel they're getting good value (and find out if they even realized you were working from home)?

If your boss feels you're still performing well you'll continue the arrangement but if he feels your work is suffering you will be prepared to end the experiment.

www.GovernmentTrainingInc.com

However, try to keep this evaluation period longer than just a couple of months – it might take the first month or two to get comfortable with your new arrangement and ramp up to your fullest productivity potential.

☐ Next, tell your boss this doesn't have to be all or nothing.

Propose to your boss that you start out by only working one or two days per week from home. Again, if things seem to be going smoothly after an agreed-upon period, you can discuss with him increasing your work-at-home days to three or more per week.

Giving your boss a chance to ease into this will make him more comfortable.

☐ Now address any remaining concerns your boss probably has about special situations where he really needs you in the office.

Your boss is probably worried about special situations. Maybe there will be a face-to-face meeting with an important customer on a day you usually work at home. Or maybe there will be a critical project on a very tight deadline that requires a couple of weeks of intense face-to-face all-day planning/coordination meetings.

Let your boss know that you will be flexible – that, when needed, you can come into the office more frequently and that you will not create dependencies on being at home on any particular day.

☐ Finally, give your boss an outline of how you plan to work at home

Detail for him what hours you expect to work, how you will be reached (e.g. you're getting a second phone line in your house just for business, you'll be forwarding your work phone to your home line), etc.

This will give your boss the confidence that you will be truly working at home and not treating work as an optional activity to fit in around the house-cleaning and watching the soaps on TV!

☐ Note: One more important thing to consider – put your plan in writing.

Perhaps your boss is amenable to the idea you proposed but needs approval from his boss before he can give you the green light.

If your proposal is written down, he can just email it to his boss and then when they discuss it, he can use it to guide the conversation. Plus, it shows his boss that you've taken this seriously and put a lot of thought into it.

Reduce the work your boss needs to do and he's more likely to be your advocate. Armed with this action-plan, it's hard to imagine your boss saying no!

Sometimes even the best-laid plans go awry:

Step 2. How do I get a job Telecommuting?

If even your well-prepared presentation does not convince your boss, don't give up completely. A 'no' now may not mean a 'no' forever.

One thing you may want to do is ask your boss, respectfully, if his refusal is due to corporate policy or due to your individual work performance.

☐ Corporate Policy

If it's corporate policy, perhaps you can find an HR person to speak to and explain the advantages previously listed for a company to let their employees telecommute – maybe the policy simply hasn't been challenged in a while.

If you have coworkers who also want to telecommute, get them to speak to HR, too.

☐ Individual Work Performance

Now if the problem is due to your individual work performance, you can tell your manager that, while you realize telecommuting is a privilege, it is important to you. Tell him you intend to redouble your efforts at work and show your manager you can do better, and maybe then he will be willing to reconsider.

Try little ways of showing him how serious you are, such as putting in some extra hours in the evening from home on that urgent report that he dropped on your desk at the last minute (which by the way, also highlights how you can successfully work from home occasionally).

Who knows, maybe the potential reward of telecommuting is just the incentive you need to kick up your work habits into a higher gear, get focused and do better!

And hey, this might just lead to improved annual performance review results, a possible increase in ranking, and a raise – all because you are fighting for something you really care about.

Proven Benefits
The benefits of a telework program are widespread. According to the International Telework Association and Council, on average, teleworking yields:
- 22 percent increase in employee productivity
- 20 percent decrease in employee turnover
- 60 percent decrease in employee absenteeism

Many senior managers have concerns about teleworking, and some of these are addressed in Appendix 1. The answers to their concerns could help persuade them that you are not only a good candidate for teleworking but that it will have a positive impact on the organization.

My Job Just Isn't Suited to Telecommuting

It is true. There are some jobs that really aren't suited to telecommuting – where you really do have to be present to do your job. Many of these are service-type jobs – how does a dentist, a policeman, or a grocery store shelf stocker telecommute? But there are many jobs that aren't quite as restrictive and can allow a little flexibility.

> **Remember:** Stop and think a little about whether you just assume you can't do your job successfully while telecommuting or if there's truly something inherent in your job that won't allow it.

Many people think that if they have lots of face-to-face meetings – perhaps working with their team to plan projects, etc. – that they can't telecommute. Well, meetings can be held by phone and the later chapters in our book even discuss how to make these kinds of meetings successful.

Others worry that if they're not in the office where people can find them, they'll be left out of decision-making and collaboration. Again, read on and learn how to overcome these possible issues.

And maybe you really do need to be present for someone. Take the executive administrator who has to be present for her boss. Probably her boss travels for business now and then and does her boss care if, on those days, his call to his admin is automatically forwarded to a different number (e.g. the second line at the admin's home)?

In fact, a recent article told about an admin who had to move away for personal reasons. She turned in her resignation but her boss insisted on keeping her because she was too valuable to him. So they set up a webcam at her house and left a monitor on her old desk (across the hall from her boss's office) showing the image from the webcam. Apparently she went back to work remotely without skipping a beat! OK, she couldn't work in her pajamas with that webcam going, but she got the rest of the benefits!

And think of the medical industry. A specialist may remotely watch a procedure or 'examine' a patient because there is no-one with the right skills on location. If doctors can work remotely, you can too!

So get creative! Even if you do need to be in the office for most of your job, perhaps you find yourself spending an hour or two per day on desk activities, such as filling in paperwork. Can you save that all up and work on it just one day per week and not come into the office that day?

Step 2. How do I get a job Telecommuting?

You are Unemployed

Well now you're starting off with a clean slate. You can stop and examine how important the option to telecommute is compared to the other wants and needs you have in your mental list for a job. Stop and prioritize it, really decide what you would or wouldn't give up for this opportunity.

Now granted, it's certainly easier to persuade a manager to let you telecommute if you've already proven yourself to him – especially if you're a top performer. There is already a level of trust developed. But that doesn't mean you have no hope. There are a few things you can do:

Research first

If telecommuting is very important to you and high on your list of requirements for your next job, stop and do some research first. Research which companies in your field are supportive, more or less, towards telecommuting.

If you don't know, ask friends at the companies you're looking at. Or call the company's Human Resources department and talk to them. Ask them roughly what percentage of the company works at least a few days per month or more from home. And how many people telecommute full-time.

Ease Into it

If you're willing to wait for your telecommuting benefit, start your new job, going into the office every day. Then, when you've been there a while, shown your abilities and proven yourself, bring up the idea of telecommuting with your boss (see the earlier part of this chapter). Of course, if it's really important that you can telecommute eventually, do some research on the company first. Perhaps even bring up telecommuting in the job interview as something you'd like to have the option to do once you've established yourself and proven yourself as an excellent performer. Of course, don't bring it up if you're not willing to lose the job offer over it.

Watch out for Scams

Be careful when you're job hunting for work that you can perform at home. There are many scams out there. If it sounds too good to be true, it probably is.

You should never have to pay to apply for a job, or pay for materials necessary to begin a job. A job is something where your employer pays you! If your potential employer says you must buy information from him to get started, move on to the next opportunity!

Consider your definition of a scam. There are jobs where you stuff envelopes. Although many people may not enjoy the job, it is not a scam.

www.GovernmentTrainingInc.com

There are other jobs where you buy parts and assemble them into products which you then return to the company for pay. However, the parts are so low quality that you cannot build a quality final product and the company refuses to pay for it. Here, most people would probably agree this is a scam.

But what if the parts are somewhat low quality, but not very low? And the company claims it has many other workers who can build the end product just fine. Is this really a scam, or just a poorly run business?

When you find what you think is a possible opportunity, research the company and see if there are complaints on the Internet about them. Think about what could possibly go wrong and ask the company about their policies. Trust your gut – if something sounds suspicious, it probably is. And if you can't trust your gut, ask around and see what other people say.

Who's Hiring

The Federal Situation

Late 20th-century technology revolutionized the workplace, and the 21st-century workplace is evolving even further. Computers, remote connectivity, voice and electronic communications, paperless work processes, and other innovations make information and work increasingly mobile.

Such innovations help the federal government, as the nation's largest employer, serve the needs of the American public more efficiently and effectively. Federal employees have used mobile work technology for a long time. In recent years, telework has become increasingly widespread and formalized, with legislative mandates, as well as new programmatic and policy supports and structures.

The Office of Personnel Management defines telework as "work arrangements in which an employee regularly performs officially assigned duties at home or other worksites geographically convenient to the residence of the employee." Telework is simply a way of getting work done from a different location. It can serve multiple purposes – and have multiple benefits – when it is implemented effectively in an organization.

For federal agencies, telework is of particular interest for its benefits in the following areas:

- ☐ Recruiting and retaining the best possible workforce – particularly newer workers who have high expectations of a technologically forward-thinking workplace and any worker who values work/life balance
- ☐ Helping employees manage long commutes and other work/life issues that, if not addressed, can have a negative impact on their effectiveness or lead to employees leaving federal employment

Step 2. How do I get a job Telecommuting?

- ☐ Reducing traffic congestion, emissions, and infrastructure impact in urban areas, thereby improving the environment
- ☐ Saving taxpayer dollars by decreasing government real estate costs
- ☐ Ensuring continuity of essential government functions in the event of national or local emergencies

Case Study: Working Together – Teleworkers and Managers

On June 10, 2009, Virginia Governor Timothy Kaine issued an Executive Order to "green" Virginia – calling for a statewide Telework Day. The Commonwealth of Virginia, Telework! VA, and Telework Exchange encouraged organizations and individuals to telework from home or a remote location on Monday August 3 – Telework Day.

The following illustrates the impact of a single day, captures feedback from participants, and demonstrates the potential for telework to deliver significant time, environmental, and cost savings.

Telework Day Snapshot: 4,267 employees teleworked on Telework Day – 22 percent of participants never teleworked before Telework Day; 95 percent of participants located in Virginia

- A Day Can Make a Difference: Telework Day participants realized significant savings – approximately $124,000 across the United States, and $113,000 in Virginia

- Want a Raise?: Teleworking one day per week delivers approximately $2,000 in savings to each teleworker annually

- Be the Change: As Telework Day demonstrated, teleworkers take cars off the road, save energy, and remove pollutants from the air. In one day, participants:
  - Avoided driving more than 155,782 miles
  - Removed 82.77 tons of pollutants from the air

- Productivity Impact: 69 percent of Virginia Telework Day participants said they accomplished more than on a typical day at the office

- Looking Forward: 91 percent of Virginia Telework Day participants said they are now more likely to telework in the future

Lessons Learned – Teleworkers Talk

What surprised you about teleworking on Telework Day?

"I knew that I could work at home, but I didn't realize that my home office environment would increase my productivity significantly."

"How apparently unprepared the ... wide area network was for handling mass remote access. I normally work at home four days per week under ADA – telecommuting day was really, really slow."

"I forwarded my office phone and answered emails promptly –surprising people at how quickly things were done. And yet I also got emails that said, "Oh, you aren't in today, I'll talk to you tomorrow." I then called people to remind them that telework means teleWORK!"

What is the most important part of successful teleworking?

"The leadership in the agency/business must fully support and encourage it."

"Ability to connect to everything you normally would be able to if sitting at your desk."

www.GovernmentTrainingInc.com

"Planning my work around teleworking, because there are some work tasks that I cannot do from home (for example, direct consumer services). I make sure that those types of tasks are covered, then schedule a 'paperwork' day at home for case management activities."

"Connectivity to coworkers/clients."

"Most important is having an environment conducive to working; i.e. quiet surroundings, ability to connect to your network, etc."

The Private Sector V Federal Sector

According to the annual CDW report, Private-sector employers have taken significant steps in the last three years to expand telecommuting programs, and private-sector telecommuting participation is approaching the federal level, with 14 percent of private-sector employees telecommuting, compared to 17 percent of federal employees. Proportionately that means there are far more teleworkers in the private sector than in the federal sector. However, federal ability to maintain business operations during a disruption continues to outpace the private sector.

Private-sector IT support has grown dramatically over the past year, with 76 percent of private-sector employers now providing technical support for remote workers, up 27 percentage points over 2007. Federal agencies remain strong advocates for telecommuting, with 56 percent of federal IT professionals indicating that their agencies provide IT support for telecommuters. Since 2005, federal IT support for telecommuting has grown 23 percent.

IT professionals in both sectors cited security as their top concern about telecommuting, with 42 percent of federal IT professionals and 27 percent of private-sector IT professionals indicating that it is their most pressing challenge. Employers are taking steps to ensure telecommuters connect securely, and most say their security procedures and systems are effective.

While continuity of operations planning (COOP) remains stronger in the federal government than in the private sector, additional emphasis on COOP plans is needed in both sectors. Fifty-nine percent of federal employees could continue to work via telecommuting if their office was closed due to a storm or other disaster, down significantly from last year, when 75 percent could continue working. The trend is reversed in the private sector, where 46 percent of employees could continue working, up 13 percentage points.

Private-sector organizations recognize they need to support a workforce that teleworks and are providing robust IT systems. Federal agencies are offering teleworkers support, but are not investing enough to support all eligible teleworkers.

Creation of a COOP plan is a critical step. All employees must know what to do in the event of an emergency. More stringent IT security requirements are controlling remote network access,

Step 2. How do I get a job Telecommuting?

contributing at least temporarily to the decline in employees who can continue their work offsite during a business disruption.

Employees want the greater work/life flexibility and productivity that telework offers, but are still concerned that management resistance will stunt their careers.

The federal government needs to continue to drive its leadership position on telework:

- ☐ Legislative requirements and lawmaker advocacy for telework
- ☐ Telework takes cars off the road, reducing gas consumption and pollution
- ☐ Military base realignment (BRAC) continues to separate skilled workers from their offices
- ☐ Aging federal workforce requires agencies to implement strategic employee-retention initiatives

Shadow Teleworking

According to the latest figures from the Office of Personnel Management, slightly more than 10 percent of eligible federal employees – or 5.72 percent of all federal employees – are teleworking. It acknowledges, however, that 22 percent of federal workers reported in 2009 that they did some 'shadow' teleworking – in most cases without formal teleworking agreements.

Some other studies suggest that the numbers might be even higher. A Telework Exchange survey in 2008 found that up to 42 percent of federal workers had teleworked at least part of the time.

The figures suggest that many employees are doing some work at home – whether on an official basis or not. They might be taking work on their personal laptops to complete a project, simply checking emails or working on complex, long-term plans. Whatever the case, if this work is being done away from the office without a formal agreement in place it poses serious security issues. Unofficial or unsanctioned work means that it is not being monitored and supervised.

If a laptop containing sensitive information is lost or stolen from an employee's home it can create a major security issue. The employee could be reluctant to report it if he or she did not have permission to have the information in the first place, which would compound the problem.

As a teleworker, you should NOT work from home or away from the main office without an agreement in place that sets out your duties and responsibilities and those of your employer. That agreement must also spell out the security procedures that have to be in place while you are teleworking to protect sensitive information and data.

Step 3. Combining Work and Family

This chapter started as a short note for insertion into another section. However, the note grew and grew as there is so much to say on this topic.

If you do not have children, and are not planning to have any in the near future you can skip this chapter. Otherwise, this is quite possibly the most important part of this book for you.

Childcare

Some people believe they can work from home while caring for kids. This false assumption is most commonly made by new parents who think they can work while caring for a small baby.

You will however quickly discover that children do not sit quietly playing with toys or books while you absorb yourself in your work. Babies and young children need ongoing attention, and you will find you get a very limited number of hours to work if you fit it in just while the kids are napping or playing quietly.

Not only that, you cannot predict when the kids will give you peace and quiet. Even if your baby naps absolutely reliably from 10-11:30 am every single day, that one day when you set up an important phone call with your boss from 10:30-11 am, your baby will somehow know and refuse to sleep during her usual naptime.

There are only two circumstances under which you should even consider caring for children while working from home:

Short and flexible hours

If you only need to work a few hours per day in your job, and the times that you work are flexible so you really can work when your child is napping.

You have older children

If your kids are older and you can work while they're in school, and in the afternoons they're relatively independent in occupying themselves at home on their homework, etc. But even then, your work really needs the flexibility in the afternoon so you can take your turn taking them to soccer practice, breaking up fights while they're supposed to be doing homework, etc.

www.GovernmentTrainingInc.com

If neither of these circumstances applies to your situation, arrange for childcare! Again, here you have two choices:

In-home care:

If you have a big enough house to close yourself in an office, and if you have enough discipline to get your work done with others in the house, a nanny may be a good solution (or recruit grandma or grandpa if you're lucky enough that they live close by and are willing to take on the work).

Personally, I loved having my children at home when they were babies. I could have them close to me, keep an eye on them and the nanny, and still get work done. I could shut myself in my office to work but take occasional breaks to visit with my baby, see if my nanny had any questions, etc. This was especially useful when the nanny was new or the baby was sick and I wanted a little extra visibility into how things were going.

Away-from-home care:

If you don't have a separate room in which you can work, or if you don't have the discipline to focus on your work when you can hear your children laughing (or crying) in the room next door, then for goodness sake, get them out of the house.

There are a number of options for away-from-home care:

- ☐ Full daycare facilities
- ☐ Home child-care programs run out of an individual's house
- ☐ A nanny-share at a friend's or neighbor's house

There is nothing hypocritical about working from home and sending your children out of the house. If you can't work in the same place as your children, there can still be advantages for the whole family for you to telecommute. You still get the time-, stress-, and money-savings of avoiding a lengthy commute, for instance. Chances are, the trip to drop the kids off at child-care out of the house is a short one.

Go back to the Advantages of Telecommuting list in Chapter 1 and determine which of these advantages you maintain. The cost savings and stress reduction alone are a benefit for the kids, too. That extra money can go into their college savings account, and what child doesn't benefit from happier, less-stressed parents?

And from the kids' perspective, once they are used to their child-care environment, they will be just as happy there as they will at home. Perhaps even happier, with a fresh set of toys and a gaggle of other children to play with and learn from. So find a child-care environment that you feel comfortable with and get to work.

Step 3. Combining Work and Family

Why Bother?

I thought I could telecommute to avoid the costs of childcare. If all my income goes into childcare costs, why not just quit my job?

This is a very good, and very important question, but the answer is not quite so obvious.

For some people, there's little to no money left from your paycheck after you pay the childcare bills. Trust me – my own paycheck is almost completely decimated paying for my son's preschool and the at-home-nanny for my baby! But there are many reasons you may choose to take this option rather than becoming a stay-at-home parent.

Temperament:

Some people are well-suited to staying at home full-time to care for the children. The opportunity to be so involved in the lives of one's children – playing with them, teaching them – can be deeply fulfilling.

However, realize that this is a tough job.

In American society, we used to ask a woman if she worked or stayed home with the kids. But lately I've noticed the language has changed and now more often than not we ask if she "works in the home" or is a "stay at home mom." Ironically, this has nothing to do with the subject of this book – telecommuting. But rather, more accurately depicts the effort of raising children.

I have done my share of being at home with the children, and I can tell you that it's a tougher job to be home all day with the kids – keeping them entertained, keeping my patience, being "on" all day, and always handling their inevitable tantrums and bad behaviors in the "right" way – than it is to have a corporate job. Yes, even with all the politics, red tape, and frustrating coworkers that come with that job!

I have the greatest respect for the women (and men) who choose to raise their children full-time because I know how tough it is.

Avoiding isolation:

> Staying home full-time with your kids can feel very isolating. You may find yourself going crazy for lack of adult interaction.
>
> *Remember*

While some parents are able to successfully create adult community in their lives through parents' groups, play-dates, etc., this takes more effort and energy than the natural interaction you automatically get with your co-workers (even when you telecommute – more on that later).

☐ Staying in the game:

I have spoken to many women who have left their jobs to raise children and once the kids are a bit older and in school, they are shocked at how hard it can be to return to the workforce. If you are out of work for more than a couple of years, your skills can become rusty, your network can crumble, and your work environment can change.

More so today than ever before, the activities one performs in a job and the tools one uses to do that job change drastically in a very short time. I've spoken to women who have told me that even the jargon in their industry has changed so much after five years that they can barely communicate intelligently with their former peers.

They may also feel like they've lost their edge and their lack of self-confidence can show through when they are interviewing for new jobs.

When these women try to return to the workforce they have to take a job that is much more junior than the one they left. And as women these days are choosing to have children later in life than they used to – after they have established their careers – starting over from the bottom is a significant loss!

So yes, the costs of childcare may suck up most of your paycheck for a few years, but in the long-run that may be less of a financial loss than the cost of having to start all over once the kids are in school.

☐ Sense of identity and self-worth:

Many people find a large chunk of their identity is tied into their career. As women choose to wait longer to have children, their pre-kid jobs are not just a temporary stint before having babies. Career is part of who they are, and how they see and value themselves.

Losing this piece of their lives can leave an unexpected hole that cannot be filled by raising children and can leave a woman feeling lost, as if some important part of herself is missing. This is doubly true for the stay-at-home-dad; men, even more than women, are judged in our society by what they do, how much they earn, etc.

Working with Dependents and Disabilities

Flexible Dependent Care

The personal freedom and flexibility of telework in turn allows for improved employee capability to care for loved ones. Essentially, those with children or ailing parents may use telework to increase their options for providing care while maintaining effective levels of work performance. This allows a person to be both employee and caretaker, removing the stress of leaving a

Step 3. Combining Work and Family

dependent entirely under the guidance of someone else, alone and unattended, or with a caregiver who may only be present for a couple of hours.

GSA published a report in August 2006 on dependent care and telework entitled, "Is Standard Practice Best Practice? Emerging Perspective on Telework and Dependent Care." The report was based on research conducted by GSA focusing on employees who were teleworking from home. GSA surveyed 1,635 federal teleworkers on their use of telework to assist with dependent-care situations. Twenty seven federal agencies and sub-agencies participated in the survey. Fifty three percent of the respondents were taking care of dependents, and of those, 91 percent indicated that telework aided them with their caretaking responsibilities. Furthermore, most of the 91 percent indicated that "telework benefited themselves as well as their dependents (happier, healthier) and their organizations (reduced turnover, improved job performance)."

Through telework, both the employer and the employee benefit from the reduced stress. Because telework allows such employees to perform their work and simultaneously have a comforting proximity to their dependents, they have lower stress levels and (possibly, depending on the circumstances) dependent care costs resulting in telework being a win-win situation for employer, caregiver, and dependent.

However, one of management's biggest concerns is that workers will be taking care of elders or children instead of doing their jobs. So specific arrangements should be spelled out before telework begins; avoiding untimely interruptions to workflow, with clear arrangements made as to specific care. For example, a babysitter may be on site while the worker is at home; or an elder might be at a senior center during working hours.

Improved Accommodations for Persons with Disabilities

One of the best potential sources of teleworkers can be found among workers with disabilities. However, not all persons with disabilities need, or want, to work at home. And not all jobs can be performed at home. But allowing an employee to work at home may be a reasonable accommodation where the person's disability prevents successfully performing the job onsite and the job, or parts of the job, can be performed at home without causing significant difficulty or expense.

In July 2010, President Barack Obama issued an executive order instructing federal agencies to increase employment of people with disabilities. The directive orders agencies to take steps to meet a goal of hiring an additional 100,000 disabled employees over five years that was originally laid out by President Clinton in a July 2000 executive order. "Few steps were taken to implement that executive order in subsequent years," said President Obama. "As the nation's largest employer, the federal government must become a model for the employment of individuals with disabilities.

Executive departments and agencies must improve their efforts to employ workers with disabilities through increased recruitment, hiring and retention of these individuals."

According to the executive order, approximately 54 million Americans are living with disabilities. President Obama said the federal government has an important interest in reducing discrimination against such Americans, in eliminating the stigma associated with disability and in encouraging Americans with disabilities to seek employment in the federal workforce.

> **Remember:** Telework improves accommodations for persons with disabilities who may prefer to work from the comfort of their home or are unable to work outside the home. While not all persons with disabilities need, or want, to work from home, telework is an option to those with reduced mobility and/or other impairment difficulties. The Bush Administration supported telework for these very benefits, stating in the President's New Freedom Initiative that the:

"Full inclusion of persons with disabilities into the workforce is an important goal not only because of the positive impact this will have on the worker, but also because of the benefits to the economy as a whole as production increases and people begin to leave government assistance … [of which may be realized by increasing] the number of employees with disabilities in the federal workforce by implementing innovative hiring and working practices, including telework …"

Jane Anderson, Executive Director for the Midwest Institute for Telecommuting Education, provided Congressional testimony on Telework for Persons with Disabilities. She said that "The National Association for the Development of Disability Research stated that the demand for telework from clients with multiple sclerosis continues to grow." Ms. Anderson provided multiple examples of telework benefiting those with disabilities and the employer – the persons with disabilities were able to work from home and the companies were not limited in their hiring. Additionally, many companies hired employees with disabilities to work off-peak hours. The persons would work evening or overnight shifts, allowing for 24-hour customer service.

Americans with Disabilities Act

In its 1999 Enforcement Guidance on Reasonable Accommodation and Undue Hardship Under the Americans with Disabilities Act (revised 10/17/02), the Equal Employment Opportunity Commission said that allowing an individual with a disability to work at home may be a form of reasonable accommodation. The Americans with Disabilities Act (ADA) requires employers with 15 or more employees to provide reasonable accommodation for qualified applicants and employees with disabilities. Reasonable accommodation is any change in the work environment or in the way things are customarily done that enables an individual with a disability to apply for a job, perform a job, or gain equal access to the benefits and privileges of a job. The ADA does not require an employer to provide a specific accommodation if it causes undue

Step 3. Combining Work and Family

hardship, such as significant difficulty or expense. Following are some commonly asked questions (and answers) about the ADA and telework.

1. **Does the ADA require employers to have telework programs?**

    No. The ADA does not require an employer to offer a telework program to all employees. However, if an employer does offer telework, it must allow employees with disabilities an equal opportunity to participate in such a program.

    In addition, the ADA's reasonable accommodation obligation, which includes modifying workplace policies, might require an employer to waive certain eligibility requirements or otherwise modify its telework program for someone with a disability who needs to work at home. For example, an employer may generally require that employees work at least one year before they are eligible to participate in a telework program. If a new employee needs to work at home because of a disability, and the job can be performed at home, then an employer may have to waive its one-year rule for this individual.

2. **May permitting an employee to work at home be a reasonable accommodation, even if the employer has no telework program?**

    Yes. Changing the location where work is performed may fall under the ADA's reasonable accommodation requirement of modifying workplace policies, even if the employer does not allow other employees to telework. However, an employer is not obligated to adopt an employee's preferred or requested accommodation and may instead offer alternate accommodations as long as they would be effective. (See Question 6.)

3. **How should an employer determine whether someone may need to work at home as a reasonable accommodation?**

    This determination should be made through a flexible "interactive process" between the employer and the individual. The process begins with a request. An individual must first inform the employer that the medical condition requires some change in the way the job is performed. The individual does not need to use special words, such as "ADA" or "reasonable accommodation" to make this request, but must let the employer know that a medical condition interferes with his/her ability to do the job.

    Then, the employer and the individual need to discuss the request so that the employer understands why the disability might necessitate the individual working at home. The individual must explain what limitations from the disability make it difficult to do the job in the workplace, and how the job could still be performed from the employee's home. The employer may request information about the individual's medical condition (including reasonable documentation) if it is unclear whether it is a "disability" as defined by the ADA. The employer and employee may wish to discuss other types of accommodations that would allow the person to remain full-time in the workplace. However, in some situations, working at home may be the only effective option for an employee with a disability.

4. **How should an employer determine whether a particular job can be performed at home?**

   An employer and employee first need to identify and review all the essential job functions. The essential functions or duties are those tasks that are fundamental to performing a specific job. An employer does not have to remove any essential job duties to permit an employee to work at home. However, it may need to reassign some minor job duties or marginal functions (such as those that are nonessential to the successful performance of a job) if they cannot be performed outside the workplace and they are the only obstacle to permitting an employee to work at home. If a marginal function needs to be reassigned, an employer may substitute another minor task that the employee with a disability could perform at home in order to keep employee workloads evenly distributed.

   After determining what functions are essential, the employer and the individual with a disability should determine whether some or all of the functions can be performed at home. For some jobs, the essential duties can only be performed in the workplace. For example, food servers, cashiers, and truck drivers cannot perform their essential duties from home. But, in many other jobs some or all of the duties can be performed at home.

   Several factors should be considered in determining the feasibility of working at home, including the employer's ability to supervise the employee adequately and whether any duties require use of certain equipment or tools that cannot be replicated at home. Other critical considerations include whether there is a need for face-to-face interaction and coordination of work with other employees; whether in-person interaction with outside colleagues, clients, or customers is necessary; and whether the position in question requires the employee to have immediate access to documents or other information located only in the workplace. An employer should not, however, deny a request to work at home as a reasonable accommodation solely because a job involves some contact and coordination with other employees. Frequently, meetings can be conducted effectively by telephone and information can be exchanged quickly through email.

   If the employer determines that some job duties must be performed in the workplace, then the employer and employee need to decide whether working part-time at home and part-time in the workplace will meet both of their needs. For example, an employee may need to meet face-to-face with clients as part of a job, but other tasks may involve reviewing documents and writing reports. Clearly, the meetings must be done in the workplace, but the employee may be able to review documents and write reports from home.

Step 3. Combining Work and Family

5. **How frequently may someone with a disability work at home as a reasonable accommodation?**

   An employee may work at home only to the extent that his/her disability necessitates it. For some people, that may mean one day a week, two half-days, or every day for a particular period of time (for example, for three months while an employee recovers from treatment or surgery related to a disability). In other instances, the nature of a disability may make it difficult to predict precisely when it will be necessary for an employee to work at home. For example, sometimes the effects of a disability become particularly severe on a periodic but irregular basis. When these flare-ups occur, they sometimes prevent an individual from getting to the workplace. In these instances, an employee might need to work at home on an "as needed" basis, if this can be done without undue hardship.

   As part of the interactive process, the employer should discuss with the individual whether the disability necessitates working at home full-time or part-time. (Some individuals may only be able to perform their jobs successfully by working at home full time.) If the disability necessitates working at home part-time, then the employer and employee should develop a schedule that meets both of their needs. Both the employer and the employee should be flexible in working out a schedule so that work is done in a timely way, since an employer does not have to lower production standards for individuals with disabilities who are working at home. The employer and employee also need to discuss how the employee will be supervised.

6. **May an employer make accommodations that enable an employee to work full-time in the workplace rather than granting a request to work at home?**

   Yes, the employer may select any effective accommodation, even if it is not the one preferred by the employee. Reasonable accommodations include adjustments or changes to the workplace, such as: providing devices or modifying equipment, making workplaces accessible (e.g., installing a ramp), restructuring jobs, modifying work schedules and policies, and providing qualified readers or sign language interpreters. An employer can provide any of these types of reasonable accommodations, or a combination of them, to permit an employee to remain in the workplace. For example, an employee with a disability who needs to use paratransit asks to work at home because the paratransit schedule does not permit the employee to arrive before 10 am, two hours after the normal starting time. An employer may allow the employee to begin his or her eight-hour shift at 10 am, rather than granting the request to work at home, if this would work with the paratransit schedule.

7. **How can employers and individuals with disabilities learn more about reasonable accommodation, including working at home?**

   Employers and individuals with disabilities wishing to learn more about working at home as a reasonable accommodation can contact the EEOC at (202) 663-4691 , (202) 663-4691 (voice) and (202) 663-7026, (202) 663-7026 (TTY). General information about reasonable accommodation can be found on EEOC's Web site, www.eeoc.gov/policy/guidance.html (Enforcement Guidance on Reasonable Accommodation and Undue Hardship Under the Americans with Disabilities Act; revised 10/17/02). This Web site also provides guidance on many other aspects of the ADA.

The government-funded Job Accommodation Network (JAN) is a free service that offers employers and individuals ideas about effective accommodations. The counselors perform individualized searches for workplace accommodations based on a job's functional requirements, the functional limitations of the individual, environmental factors, and other pertinent information. JAN can be reached at 800-526-7234, 800-526-7234 (voice or TDD); or at www.jan.wvu.edu/soar.

STEP 4. THE HOME OFFICE

Since you're still reading at this point it means you have a strong feel that telecommuting is a valid option for you. So let's start talking about what you need to be successful.

> The first thing is to make sure you have the setup and tools at home to do your job. We will discuss each item in some detail in the following sections. However, this book will only describe what you need.

Must Do

There are many books and resources available on the details of how to get these items, comparing costs, quality, etc.

Your 'Office'

Let's talk first about the space you'll need; somewhere that you can go to be left alone and get your work done. If you're fortunate, you'll have enough room in your house to have an office dedicated to your work where you can shut the door and focus. If you're very lucky that room will be far away from the center of the house and any distractions.

However, we do not all live in an ideal world. You may need to have your desk in an open part of the house – a corner of the living room for instance. You will have to examine your needs carefully to determine what will work for you.

If you live alone or with a spouse who is out of the house all day:

In this quieter living environment, you may not need to shut yourself away behind a door. You may be able to work at the kitchen table for example. However, if you plan to do so make sure at a minimum that you clean up the table the night before so you aren't trying to work around dirty dishes and other distractions.

Remember, this is where you'll be doing the job that brings in your income to pay your bills. Create the environment you need to focus and perform exceptionally.

If there are other people in the house while you are working:

On the other hand, if there will be other people in the house, especially if there are children at home, you absolutely need to find a way to create some privacy. But that doesn't mean you need a big, fancy office.

www.GovernmentTrainingInc.com

Telework: How to Telecommute Successfully

My own desk is in a closet! In my house, we do not have the space we'd ideally like. We have one small room that has to fit my desk and my husband's, a guest bed, plus the bookshelf, file cabinets, etc. One way we achieved this was to take the doors off the closet, remove all the junk from there, and put my desk inside. It fits nicely and gives us the extra few square feet of space we need.

Yes, there's a little less storage space, but it's not as if I need to hang clothes in there! I bought a bunch of those clear boxes (that come in sizes similar to a shoe box and bigger) that you can get from your local Target, Wal-Mart, or closet organizer store, and you'd be amazed at how much stuff I can store in those and keep on the upper shelves of the closet above my desk.

A futon opens up into a guest bed as needed. Fortunately my guests understand and don't complain about the cramped space. And thank goodness for portable laptops and wireless networks so if I have a 7:00 am meeting the next day, I can take it in my own bedroom without disturbing the guests!

> **Tips**
> Even if you don't have a separate room for an office at all, get creative. Perhaps you can fit a desk in your bedroom. Or perhaps you can put up an interior wall with a door to close off the dining room. This may not appeal to your aesthetic ideal for your house, but you have to determine what your priorities are. How important is it for you to telecommute successfully? You cannot be on an important phone meeting with your boss or coworkers with small children shrieking in the background or trying to climb on you and pull on the phone.

Ergonomics

Now that you have your space defined, you need to realize that you will be spending many hours here. Just as it is important in the company office to make sure your ergonomics are sound, so too is this important in your home.

In fact, it may be even more important; where in the company office you got up from your desk often to attend meetings in conference rooms and chat with your co-worker down the hall, at home all these meetings and chats are taking place from your desk chair.

Often in large companies, fully adjustable-height desks, fancy ergonomic chairs, etc., are the norm. At home you may not have the resources to buy top-of-the-line office equipment. But there are cheap options to make your life easier.

Desk and chair height:

This is important – when you sit in your chair your knees should be bent at a 90-degree angle with your feet resting flat on the floor. Your elbows should be open just slightly more than 90 degrees with your wrists straight and your fingertips resting gently on the keyboard.

Step 4. The Home Office

Well that's great if you happen to be the perfect proportions for the desk height you have. But otherwise do you have to go out and buy an expensive desk that's got an adjustable height option? Surely, if you're a full-time telecommuter, that's the only solution.

WRONG!

My desk consists of an old door laid on its side, and supported under one end by a file cabinet and the other by a set of drawers with an old dictionary on top (because the drawers are shorter than the file cabinet). I love it because the door is thick and rock solid, and I would have a hard time fitting my file cabinet in my office otherwise (my husband's desk and ever-growing unread book collection fills the rest of the room).

My chair, on the other hand is pretty fancy with adjustments for height, base tilt, back tilt, etc. My husband found it along with his own chair at a surplus-office-supply store. Cost: $50 total for both chairs! Yes there's a small tear on the arm of the chair, but next to my desk I'm not exactly worried about it looking pretty!

Even with the fancy chair cranked up to full height, I'm not quite high enough. So I sit on a small pillow. However, now my feet are dangling inches off the ground – putting pressure on my thighs and, thank-you, but I do not want to encourage varicose veins! So I've taken an old box, from one of my husband's trips to Fry's Electronics, which is about four inches tall and put it under my desk. My feet rest comfortably on that, and now I'm in perfect ergonomic arrangement.

Monitor Height:

Your monitor should be quite high up so your eyes are roughly at the level somewhere between the top of the screen and about 1/3 down the screen.

However, I don't even have a separate monitor. I have a stack of old books on my desk and my laptop sits on top of these so the monitor is just the right height.

I have a separate keyboard and mouse that I plug in so I'm not actually touching the laptop (which would be too high, plus it's balanced pretty precariously on that pile of books!). Again great ergonomics, and all I paid for out of my pocket for this piece was the keyboard and mouse.

Keyboard and Mouse:

Once more, I will remind you that you'll be spending more time sitting in front of your computer when you telecommute so you really do have to get all the ergonomics right.

I learned an interesting ergonomics tidbit that is especially useful for women or shorter men:

Most people put their mouse on the right side of their keyboard (if you're right handed). However, notice that on most keyboards the right side has all the extra keys beyond the standard alphabet section – there's the number pad, the direction keys, etc. So this means you have a long stretch from where you are sitting in front of the 'home' keys on the keyboard to reach your mouse. For women who typically have shorter arms, and even for many men, this forces you to reach your arm out pretty far – not a good ergonomic position to be sitting in hour after hour. So you have two options:

1. **Buy a compact keyboard.**

These are easy to find and only extend the keyboard a couple of inches past the basic alphabetic character keys. They typically combine the number pad with the directional keys.

2. **Try mousing left-handed.**

Impossible you say? I tried switching my mouse many years ago and yes, at first it felt very awkward. But I assure you that if you force yourself to use your mouse left-handed for two solid days it will begin to feel quite natural. And it's especially handy if you do much data entry with the number keypad, as your right hand is now completely free.

Plus, you have the added bonus that for the rest of your life you can mouse with either hand – making it easy when you're at a friend's house and need to look something up online – whether that friend is a Righty or a Lefty! On a more serious note, if you're doing a lot of mouse work for a few days and that arm begins to get sore, you have the added advantage of being able to switch to the other arm. I tend to switch my mouse from one side to the other every month or so just to keep myself balanced.

Please note that I am not a trained ergonomic specialist. The above tips and information are based on my own personal experience and are not a complete list. Your own needs may vary, so please take the time to make sure you are completely comfortable at your desk – and do some searching around online for more information if anything doesn't feel quite right.

There are many resources on office ergonomics (see my Web site at http://nicolebachelor.com for some good links). Make sure you take the time to set yourself up properly – you do not want to suffer the inevitable backaches, headaches, and repetitive stress injuries that come from a poor office setup.

Hardware and Connectivity

Your Computer:

If you're lucky, your company has provided you (or you can ask for) a laptop that you can do your work on. If that's the case, then you've got what you really need to get started.

Step 4. The Home Office

I would, however, advise getting a monitor and/or a keyboard/mouse so you can create a more ergonomically friendly environment (see the previous section on ergonomics). You do not want to be spending eight-plus hours a day hunched over a laptop and the small keyboard and monitor that comes with it.

If you cannot get a laptop from your company, you will have to consider purchasing your own computer. The choice of what kind of computer (desktop vs. laptop, powerful vs. affordable, etc.) depends entirely on what you need to do for work and what other personal tasks you want to perform on this computer. Check online for resources that can help you make a decision.

> Tip: If you do use your own personal computer for work, be sure to keep your work and personal folders, files, etc., separated so they don't get mixed up.
>
> When you're working you need to be able to find your documents quickly and easily, and the last thing you need is to accidentally send your boss your personal finance spreadsheet instead of your work finance spreadsheet!!!
>
> Have one root folder on your computer for work documents, and keep all work-related items in sub-folders under that.

Internet and Intranet Access:

First, if your job involves a lot of email and accessing documents online, you absolutely need a fast, reliable Internet connection. No phone dialup lines here – you need to be able to work just as quickly and efficiently as when you are in the office.

So pay for a service provider, such as your phone company or cable company, to provide you with good quality Internet access. And if you don't know your best option, check online resources!

Note that this is not the end of the work needed to access your company's intranet (the network within the company that's not visible to the outside world). They will have firewalls set up to protect their security so that you can't access your company email and important documents with Internet access alone.

You will need to talk to your IT department about how to gain access. Most companies have a VPN (Virtual Private Network) that allows you to "tunnel" into the corporate firewall and gain the access you need.

However, in a very small company you might need to make some special arrangements and this, in itself, can become a hurdle to getting the full green light on telecommuting.

Someone could write a book on this subject alone, as there are so many possible arrangements here, but I am not an expert on the technical details. Talk to your IT folks and if they don't have something already set up, prepare to roll up your sleeves and do a little digging for assistance (or sweet-talk the IT guy into helping you).

Telework: How to Telecommute Successfully

> **Tip:** Don't forget to follow all your company's security rules and regulations when it comes to protecting your computer, your company's intellectual property, and your network connection to your company. When working from home, there is increased risk that important information could become compromised – don't make your company regret their telecommuting policies.

Your Phone and Phone Line:

Since you're working at home, all those face-to-face meetings and even hallway chats must be replaced now by phone calls. This means you're going to be on the phone a lot more than you were when you went into the company office.

So you're going to need to think carefully about what phone line you use. Can you just use your regular home line? Perhaps, but this depends on who else is around.

- ☐ Do you have children at home who are likely to answer the phone when your boss is calling you?
- ☐ Do you have a spouse at home who might pick up and start dialing without realizing that you're in the middle of an important meeting?
- ☐ Do you set a peppy outgoing answering machine message that has dogs barking to the tune of Jingle Bells around the holiday season?

If you answered yes to any of the above, you should probably get a second line in your home for work.

This becomes more important the more days a week you plan to telecommute. Some people who only work at home occasionally choose to just check their work voicemail a few times throughout the day and not worry about second phone lines or forwarding their phone.

But this means people can never reach you directly by calling and this is a big disadvantage if you are telecommuting full-time or even frequently. Remember, people's access to you is already restricted because they can't see you or wander over to your cubicle/office.

So make sure it's easy for people to reach you by phone! There are cheap, and even free, second phone line options out there. Just do a little digging around online for resources and recommendations to see what best meets your needs and budget.

Extra Features:

A second phone line has the added benefit that you can get voicemail on this phone line and set a professional outgoing message for when you can't answer the line. And you probably want to get Caller ID and Call Waiting which you most likely have at the company office, too.

Step 4. The Home Office

If your company phone system has the capability, forward your company phone number to your second home line on the days you telecommute. Alternately, if your company lets you, you can switch the phone number listed in the corporate directory to your second home line and use this going forward as your main work number – especially if you are telecommuting full-time, or nearly full-time, and plan to do so indefinitely.

Headset:

Along with the phone line you need a headset. As I said, you'll be spending more hours on the phone than you are used to and you'll probably be typing notes, etc., as you talk. You don't want to end up with a stiff neck and headaches from propping your handset between your ear and shoulder.

And, when you get a headset make sure it (or the phone you're connecting it to) has a mute button. This is critical!

You do not want to have background household noises interrupting your phone calls. It is unprofessional and, depending on the interruption (especially those of you with toddlers at home), can be quite embarrassing!

Also, while your manager and co-workers may be fine with you telecommuting, they don't need constant reminders from the background noise. Company offices are typically very quiet. Even the layout and furnishings are designed to swallow up noise – the materials used on the floors, ceilings, and even the walls of the cubicles are often soft sound-absorbing materials rather than hard noise-reflecting surfaces.

And even for those of you who live alone, all it takes is for your neighbors to have construction going on or be mowing their lawn, and you need that mute switch.

I've found myself in this situation occasionally – where there's a loud ongoing noise outside my house while I'm on a phone conference. That mute switch has saved my life. I keep the phone on mute until the moment I have something to say, flip the switch, speak, and flip it back again. Even if I'm in a conversation, I'll turn the mute on and off continuously if I have to.

Although some phone conference tools have the ability to let you type a sequence of buttons to mute and unmute, do you really want to be typing *64 and *63 over and over again as you speak?

Peripherals (Printer, Fax Machine, Scanner):

Finally, spend a moment to think about any office peripherals you may need, such as a printer. You may not need this on day one of your telecommuting experience, but you may find over time you need one.

This depends on the type of work you do and how often (if ever) you go into your office. If you don't often have to print and you go into your office once a week, you may not need a printer at home. But if you need to print long documents regularly and telecommute full-time, getting a good quality, high-speed printer may be a must for you.

While you're at it, consider if you will need related tools, such as a fax machine or scanner. These days you can get one piece of equipment that can perform three tasks. This will save you a bit of money, as well as a lot of desk space! Again, there are many resources online that provide great information on the different costs and options for office peripherals.

Step 5: Working at Home

Now you're all set – you have your telecommuting agreement arranged, you've got a nice space set up in a home office or other corner of the house to work, you have your internet access, phone line, computer, etc all ready to go.

Now what?

Now you just get to work – business as usual – you're set to go?

No – Not Exactly!

> This is the part where many people fall down. They just assume that working at home is exactly the same as working in the office and they just need to get to it. However, there are subtle but significant differences that now have to be addressed if you want to be truly successful as a telecommuter.

Remember

So, what's different?

Well you are no longer right next to your boss and co-workers. Although this has some of the advantages listed in the beginning of this book (less interruptions due to workplace gossip, etc.) it also has some big disadvantages you need to properly manage.

Out-of-sight, Out-of-mind

When your boss needs extra help on a quick project, he's going to go to the person he thinks of first. And chances are that's the first person who falls into his line of sight.

While at first you may be relieved to no longer be interrupted to help out here and there, over the long haul it's these little things you do to help out that get you noticed and play a part in the advancement of your career.

Let's take another example. Your coworkers are working on a project that impacts one of your projects. When you're right there and they're talking about it you might overhear the discussion and join in. Or they see you and remember to pull you in. But when you're not around, you can easily be overlooked. Now activities are going on around you that you don't have awareness of and therefore you don't step in to make sure your own needs are represented.

Here's another example. Let's take the employee who is often sought after for advice or input. Perhaps he has a long history with the team/projects or maybe has a good handle on the

www.GovernmentTrainingInc.com

interdependencies between the different activities and products in the organization. You know – the guy everyone tends to check in with or run things by because he always is aware of something that you hadn't considered.

Again, on the one hand he may be relieved to have less interruptions when he telecommutes so he can get "his own work" done.

But what he may be overlooking was that being the team go-to guy was a big part of "his own work". This is where his coworkers and even his boss really valued him and is part of why he got the high rankings and good pay raises. Suddenly this is gone and although it may not show up immediately, over time this added value erodes and he suddenly wakes up one day to an average ranking and no pay raise for the year.

The out-of-sight-out-of-mind phenomenon is a gradual, less obvious problem that many people overlook because it's not noticeable at first.

Over time, it can erode your previously successful career. You can start becoming more isolated, losing the visibility of what your peers are doing while they lose visibility of what you're doing. The synergies in your projects disappear so down the road your services/products don't interconnect so well with related ones.

Not only that, but since your coworkers don't see you, they start somehow feeling that you're not working as much as they are and resentments can start to build.

Remember
This is the difference between "telecommuting" and "telecommuting successfully". When you telecommute successfully, you maintain your virtual presence so people are more aware of you. They work closely with you on related projects, come to you frequently with questions, and include you in decision-making. And your boss asks for your involvement and thinks of you when it's time to give out those raises and promotions!

Plan the Work
Employees who telework should assess the portability of their work and the level of technology available at the remote location. They will need to plan their telework days to be as productive as possible by considering the following questions:
- What files, documents, and equipment will I need to take when I leave my regular workplace the day before teleworking?
- Who needs to be notified that I will be teleworking?
- What other steps should I take before leaving the office (e.g., forwarding the phone)?
- In the case of emergency telework, what should I have available at all times at my home office or, if applicable, a telework center, to enable me to be functional without coming onsite to retrieve materials?

Step 5. Working at home

Manage Expectations and Communication

Managers are ultimately responsible for the effective functioning of the workgroup. Nevertheless, to avoid any negative impact from their arrangement, teleworkers should help manage the group's expectations and their own communication. Issues that should be addressed include the following:

Backup: Even with very portable work there are inevitably instances where physical presence is required and a coworker may need to step in. Coworker backup should be planned, reasonable, and reciprocal. Cross-training of staff has broad organizational benefits and should be a management priority.

On-the-spot assistance: Teleworkers may occasionally need someone who is physically in the main office to assist them (e.g., to fax a document or look up information). Again, these arrangements should not be unduly burdensome; a "buddy system" between teleworkers may be the most feasible solution. For example, if one teleworker needs a document or piece of office equipment, he or she can contact another teleworker (or the manager) who is in the office that day and arrange for a pickup at a mutually convenient location. The favor will be reciprocated as needed.

Communication with manager: The manager must be kept apprised of the teleworker's schedule, how to make contact with the teleworker, and the status of all pending work.

Communication with coworkers: Coworkers must be informed about the appropriate handling of the teleworker's telephone calls or other communications.

Communication Styles

Successful communication is a very necessary part of any job. And with telecommuting comes a change in your communications. Communicating remotely, by phone or email, is quite different from face-to-face communication.

"The greatest problem of communication is the illusion that it has been accomplished." ~ George Bernard Shaw

This quote really drives home the dangers with any type of unsuccessful communications. And remote communications can be even trickier, and even more likely to cause the illusion that they have succeeded, than face-to-face communications.

Modes of Communication

Let's start by discussing how we communicate. When you're in the office, there are many casual, quick face-to-face encounters.

But what happens when you're telecommuting and you have a quick question or need a little information? You can't just stand up, peak over the cubicle wall, check if your coworker is on the phone and, if not, have a short conversation about the topic at hand. Instead you have to pick up the phone and hope your coworker will answer.

Let's face it, we treat phones differently than we treat people. When you're deeply engrossed in your work and the phone rings, chances are you might just let voicemail pick up (or hope they hang up and go bother someone else instead). But if someone hovers outside your cubicle, social etiquette dictates that you politely stop what you're doing and give this intruder your full attention.

www.GovernmentTrainingInc.com

Successful telecommuters have other techniques and methods to get the information they need as quickly and easily as those people who always go into the office.

Communicating without Visual Cues

Also consider how you operate at a meeting. Let's say you've called together a meeting and, while presenting the information that you need your teammates to discuss, you notice half of them are yawning, typing on their laptops, or pulling out their cell phones to play Minesweeper.

Or perhaps you notice that your teammates are looking at you with puzzled expressions, scratching their heads, or leaning over to whisper questions to the person next to them.

Either way, clearly you've lost your audience, and you have to change tactics or re-double your efforts to get them involved.

Now remove all those visual cues and imagine how the same meeting will go. You may continue plowing along, slide after slide, having no idea that your audience is no longer following you. And when the meeting is over the whole purpose of bringing these people together has been wasted.

The fact is that we get a significant amount of information from the people we talk to from their body language. This is not just true for meetings (although it may be more significant then) – it even applies to the casual conversation you have with your coworker or boss in the hallway.

A successful telecommuter who deals with his peers and manager remotely has techniques and methods for dealing with this absence.

Improving Your Virtual Presence

Clearly, falling victim to the Out-of-Sight-Out-of-Mind phenomenon is dangerous for any career. And combined with the required changes in communication styles, you can see how people who don't think telecommuting requires any changes compared to going into the office will surely fail.

The good news is there are many solutions to help address these challenges. In general, you need ways to increase your virtual presence as a replacement for your physical presence. Get yourself back into your coworkers' and manager's minds even if you're not in their sights.

> **Must Do:** The keys to thwarting the out-of-sight-out-of-mind phenomenon is to make sure you know what your peers are doing, they know what you're doing, and you can all reach each other quickly and easily.

There are a number of tools available to help you communicate with your team members and stay at the front of their minds: Email, Instant Messenger, Phone, Web Meeting/Collaboration

Step 5. Working at home

solutions. As is the case with all tools, there are better and worse ways to use them. The next few chapters will focus on each of these tools in turn and provide you with tips and techniques to use them to their best effect.

> Tip: Everyone operates differently. You may find that what works well for one coworker does not for another. If you find some people are more comfortable interacting by phone and others by email, be flexible. And if you can, remember who prefers what and use the right tool for the right person. It is in your best interest to communicate as effectively as possible with everyone with whom you work.

The Phone

Ah, the phone. By far the oldest of our "high tech" forms of communication, the phone is also our closest replacement to actually being there in person. It is probably the fastest of our remote communication tools (most people can talk faster than they type) and unlike email and Instant Messaging, you still get a lot of information (above and beyond the actual words spoken) from tone of voice, etc.

Of course, everyone (I hope) knows how to use a phone. And even non-telecommuters use the phone frequently in their day-to-day jobs. But for non-telecommuters the phone is a secondary form of communication (getting up and walking over to a coworker's desk is the primary method).

Therefore, the importance of mastering highly effective phone skills is critical to a telecommuter who must use the phone as one of their primary communication modes. There are a lot of techniques a successful telecommuter utilizes to make their phone communications more effective and to increase their virtual presence.

One-on-One Phone Meetings

A Real-Life Story

In my telecommuting experience, I had a coworker (let's call him Bob) who was a real character. Bob was very no-nonsense, was good at what he did and knew it, had a very dry, sarcastic wit (it was often hard to tell if he was joking or serious), and was no-holds-barred with his comments and opinions.

Bob could be difficult to work with, but he was the engineer on my product and I needed to have a good relationship with him.

A few others had found that the best way to work with Bob was to go out with him for beers after the workday, and then he would start talking. It was apparently much easier to pick Bob's brain, get the info you needed, initiate conversations, etc., this way.

Unfortunately I hate beer and also didn't live in the same state as Bob did, so going out for beers with him was a problem.

One of the reasons Bob behaved the way he did was that since he was a very good engineer, he always had so much work on his plate. There were huge dependencies on Bob to get code written for critical projects that had tight timelines. He was under a lot of pressure and did not have much time. So any time he had to "waste" chatting with his project managers, filling in status updates, etc., made him grouchy.

My solution came when I was chatting with a mutual coworker. He suggested I needed to establish a more predictable method to get my information without causing unexpected interruptions or anything that might appear to "make work" for Bob.

So I decided to set up a short, regularly-scheduled phone meeting. It was only for a ½ hour and only every other week. This showed Bob that I was not trying to waste his time and that my interruptions of his work were being kept to a minimum.

During the periods between our meetings, whenever a question came up that I needed Bob's input on, I carefully scrutinized whether or not it could wait until our next meeting. Often it could. If so, I put a note on my "Bob list."

When my next meeting came up I would go through my "Bob list" and bang out all the questions. Often I could go through a number of topics with him very quickly, and we could be done with our meeting well before the ½ hour was up.

On the times that I didn't have anything on my "Bob list," I'd send Bob a quick note earlier in the day to tell him I had nothing for him and unless he needed something from me we could cancel the meeting, and he could get that ½ hour back.

This arrangement worked well. Bob started to trust that I was not going to waste his time. Also, since Bob was a bit of a gossip, I would typically spend the first five minutes or so chit-chatting with him about the latest corporate politics and management shenanigans. He liked this because he got to vent about whatever was going on and he knew, since we only had ½ hour and I was always careful not to go longer – if I had too many questions I held the less urgent ones for our next meeting, our chatting would not extend the amount of time he was pulled away from his "real work."

Our relationship improved drastically, and I found myself working very well with Bob.

A Real-Life Story – Part II

Now, that story sounds pretty good, pretty convincing right?

Step 5. Working at home

But I know there's always a skeptic out there (because I'm usually that person) who isn't fully convinced. Could these meetings really have made such a difference?

Well, one could suppose that my meetings were not necessarily the cause of the improvement. Perhaps Bob's boss had also recently told him that he needed to improve his attitude towards his coworkers and my meetings were just a coincidence.

However, after a while I left for maternity leave to have my second child. On my return, I'd dropped all the meetings on my calendar. And I'd forgotten about my regular meetings with Bob. Having babies and the associated sleep deprivation can do a little long-term damage to one's memory.

After a while I found my relationship with Bob had deteriorated and I was struggling again to get the information I needed from him and work with him successfully. One day, I remembered our old meetings and I immediately set them up again. Within a short time, Bob seemed happier to work with me again, our relationship was easier, and life was good.

The lesson here is to find some structured, regularly recurring way to get a little one-on-one time with those with whom you work. This gives you a chance to connect and strengthen your relationship, to keep your coworkers abreast of what you're working on (and vice versa), and to knock out the questions that crop up here and there in a very efficient manner.

Tip: Although this section is about one-on-one phone meetings, you may also want to consider more frequent team phone meetings.

If you were used to getting your team together to meet every other week to compare notes and provide status, consider making these weekly.

What you may not consciously notice when you're in the office is that there are probably at least weekly occurrences when a few members of the team start talking about the project, and the rest of the team either joins in or just absorbs the conversation from their seats. When you are telecommuting, you do not learn the information that comes out of these casual exchanges of ideas, and a slightly more frequent recurring meeting can help take their place.

Phone Meetings With Your Manager

One-on-one phone meetings are a very critical part of your interactions when you work remotely. The most common and important of these meetings are those with your manager.

Many managers schedule weekly or biweekly meetings with each of their direct reports, to check in and discuss whatever issues have been cropping up, to make sure the employee is on track and prioritize the right tasks, etc.

If your office is right next door to your manager's you may find you don't need these regularly scheduled meetings, as you see him frequently enough to discuss all the miscellaneous items as they crop up. But when you telecommute, these meetings become critical. If you don't already have these arranged, speak to your boss. Ask him if you can set something up to help ensure that you keep the lines of communication open.

If you already have such a meeting set up, the next challenge is to keep it. Managers are often very busy and frequently get pulled into emergency or urgent situations that they cannot avoid. As a result, they are notorious for canceling these one-on-one meetings. They figure, of all their meetings, these are the most flexible (it only affects one other person and it's not for a particular urgent topic, etc.).

While this may be true, and an occasional cancellation is not a big deal, you must make sure this doesn't become a pattern. I have had managers who would cancel almost every one-on-one meeting, week after week, due to one urgent issue after another. When you work from home, these meetings are often your only opportunity to discuss important issues with your manager.

So if you see this pattern, try to stop it. Talk to your manager (when you can finally get a moment of his time). Explain why these meetings are important to you. If he has to cancel, immediately try to reschedule for later that day or later that week. Your manager is busy, so you must be the one to remain vigilant and keep pushing for his time (politely of course).

Keeping the Attention During Phone Calls

Have you ever been talking on a phone call and all you get back is the occasional "mm-hmm …" now and then? And then you finally stop talking and expect a response and there's just a long silence?

I had this happen frequently with one manager. I'd be giving him a brain dump on some issue or situation on which I needed his input, and at the end of my little speech there would be dead silence. I'd have to prompt him for an answer and coach him through what I'd just finished telling him.

We all know in these cases what's going on. The person on the other end of the phone is only half listening to you and simultaneously working on emails or talking to someone else on IM or whatever.

This can be a very frustrating experience – and very counterproductive to the whole purpose of the phone call. Unfortunately this is a situation that's really affected by the lack of physical presence. If you were standing at the person's cubicle talking to them, you can be quite sure (unless the person is unusually rude) that they would never dream of reading emails or talking to other people over IM while you're talking.

This is a situation where the person on the other end of the phone performs the other activities because they can. Chances are they are not choosing to work on other tasks because they

Step 5. Working at home

think what you have to say isn't important. It's more likely that they're horribly overloaded (as we all are these days) and are just trying to squeeze in a quick answer to a short email, which turns into addressing another email, and another.

You really need to be proactive to prevent these situations. You will probably get a good sense for which people are more likely to do this to you (again, don't take it personally – they probably do it to everyone). For these people, here are some ideas to try:

Keep them engaged:

Don't talk for a long time without letting the person on the other end of the phone respond. In fact, force them to respond frequently.

Choose your language so instead of saying "I think this approach is best for our project" you can say something like "I think this approach is best for our project, do you agree?" If they are constantly being forced to respond to your conversation, they will give up trying to do other activities at the same time.

Find other ways to communicate:

Some people just do better with different communication styles than others. Perhaps this person is better with email than phone? Try explaining the issue in an email and let them respond that way.

Or, sometimes I have written up a message explaining a situation and hit "Send" right before my scheduled one-on-one phone call. Then when I speak to the person by phone, I will tell them I had already written up the issue and that it's probably easier for them to read it than have me try to explain it. I ask them to read it over while we're on the phone and just wait silently while they read. At least this way there's no way they can be working on other emails while they're reading your message.

Be blunt (politely):

As I said, I had a manager who was awful about not listening during our one-on-one phone calls. I had lived with it, re-explaining things as necessary when he got caught unable to answer a question. But I had something very important I needed to discuss with him one day.

I very politely told him that this matter was very important and I know how we all can be distracted by emails and IMs, so would he mind possibly switching his monitor off and I would do the same to make sure we had a focused conversation.

We had a pretty good relationship and he was pretty forthright about his own behaviors, so he made some joking comment back about how I was asking him to quit ignoring me like he usually did. But even if he hadn't liked the implication, he could have saved face by not acknowledging he personally had a problem with this (I had phrased my request to keep it generic and imply this was an issue many people including myself had).

Along these same lines, don't be the one to cause this problem for others. If you're constantly working on other tasks while your co-workers are trying to talk to you, pretty soon they'll decide that working with you when you're at home is too hard, and they'll just stop communicating.

This is not their problem – it is your problem. You are the one who wants to telecommute and ultimately with that lack of communication from your co-workers, you are the one whose work will suffer.

If this means that when you're on the phone you need to switch off your monitor or close down your email application then do it!

Email

Like the telephone, email is another tool to help you with your communications and virtual presence.

Email is a complicated beast. Unlike the telephone which is used for simple conversations or group discussions, email serves a wide variety of purposes. Here's a short list of just some of the ways email can be used:

- ☐ To include a group in a conversation
- ☐ To discuss a topic in great detail
- ☐ To provide directions/instructions or set expectations
- ☐ To capture information that needs to be passed around or used in the future
- ☐ To provide a formal commitment
- ☐ To capture a discussion and save it for later use – often for political reasons
- ☐ To continue a conversation over an extended time period

As a result, there are many more aspects to consider when using email.

Must Do

Since the telecommuter uses this tool more than the non-telecommuter who can have live face-to-face conversations with coworkers, the telecommuter needs to know all the best techniques to use email to his best advantage.

The Single Most Important Lesson When Using Email

I've learned this one the hard way a few times, and probably will still make the same mistake occasionally in my career. But if I could provide only one single piece of advice about email it would be …

Step 5. Working at home

Do not put anything into an email that you would not be willing to have publicly forwarded to anybody you can think of (including your boss, your peers, your clients, your competitors, your spouse, your friends, etc.).

I can't stress this lesson enough. Let me give you just two of my own personal real-life examples to highlight what I'm saying.

1. I was upset at a situation with a friend of mine. I can't even remember the details, but she wrote me an email about something related to the situation and, for whatever reason, what she wrote just made me angrier. I needed to vent, so I forwarded her message to my husband and wrote exactly how I felt about her and how I perceived she had wronged me.

Well, about two seconds after I hit the "Send" button, I realized that instead of forwarding the message to my husband, I had used the "Reply" button. The message I'd intended for my husband's eyes only had gone right back to my friend.

I was horrified but it was too late. Within about five minutes I got a reply from her where she was obviously quite upset. I explained that this had been a mistake and I hadn't intended for her to see what I had written, but obviously that didn't really make her feel much better.

Well the good news is we smoothed things over, but I learned a hard lesson that day.

2. Many years later, long after I'd forgotten about the previous story, I made another mistake. I had written a request for information to a couple of coworkers. I knew one of these coworkers wasn't very reliable about responding in a timely manner. So I wrote the request in a rather aggressive tone.

I followed up with a separate message to the other coworker (the one I trusted more) explaining that the tone had not been aimed at her but rather at the other guy who I knew she understood wasn't that reliable.

Well, she forwarded that message (the second one with the private explanation) to our boss because of some other information in it that she wanted him to see. He replied back to her with an answer and then she took his reply and forwarded it to a whole group of our mutual team members so they could see the conversation. It had nothing to do with what I had written, but if you scrolled down a few conversations in the email thread, you could see what I had said.

I realized it was quite likely that some of those teammates would further continue the conversation, and this email thread could end up circling right around to the coworker who had been the brunt of my somewhat derogatory comments in the first place!

I had to "Reply All" and ask everyone to please not further send out the message due to what I had written earlier in the thread.

Fortunately, the conversation seemed to die shortly thereafter, but it was just luck that it didn't continue further. And even with my request for people not to forward the conversation further, not everyone reads all the emails in their inbox before acting on some of the earlier ones. I got lucky that day.

As you can see, there are too many possibilities for something you write, through your own error or simply an oversight on someone else's part, to fall into the wrong people's hands.

Do not write anything in an email if you would be upset to have certain other people read it. In the second example, I would have been better calling my coworker (the one I trusted) and explaining my first message to her that way.

> Tips
> Tip: Another reason to be careful about what you write in an email is, like physical letters, emails can be subpoenaed for their content in a court of law. Be careful what you write. Follow your company policies about how long you are allowed to archive old messages – some companies do not like to have their employees storing email messages for too long.

Make Your Message Clear

This is a big area to discuss. Consider how many emails you get every day – dozens, hundreds?

It's hard to find time to read and respond to all of them, especially when this is not the core aspect of your job and you have "real work" to do!

The biggest thing someone can do to make your life easier is to make their emails to you as clear, concise, and simple as possible. Besides the increased respect you will have for them, you will also be more likely to understand exactly what they are asking and provide the requested information, which means they get what they need.

So let's look at some techniques for this:

Email Subject:

The subject of the email message is the first thing the person sees and in some cases may be all they look at before they hit the delete button. Yow!

So the subject of your message has to get across the main point of your communication and exactly what you need the reader to do about it.

The best way to do this is to use tags with your email message. A tag is a brief phrase immediately before the true message subject that indicates to the reader what you want from them. Some common tags are –

☐ FYI:

Step 5. Working at home

☐ Action Required:

☐ For Your Approval:

☐ Confirmation Requested:

☐ Urgent Response Needed:

As you can see, these tags clearly tell the reader if you expect some kind of action from them or not. While you may feel like the body of the message clearly tells the person this information, remember that busy people often briefly scan email messages and if you have already set their expectations on what you need them to do with it, they'll more likely spot the actual question or request within the message body.

Follow the tag with the main subject of the message. Ask yourself what's the point of the message you're sending and the answer is your subject. Can you get the main summary of what the message body is about into 10 words or less?

Below are some examples of email subjects that use tags and clearly explain the purpose of the message. In each case, you should clearly be able to tell what is expected of the reader:

☐ **FYI:** New process for submitting reimbursement requests

☐ **Action Required:** Submit next year's budget needs by November 15

☐ **For your approval:** Proposal on ABC Widget project scope

☐ **Confirmation requested:** Can we move forwards with beta test?

☐ **Urgent, response needed:** Need info for customer quote due by end of day

Email Body:

I could write a book on this section alone. Probably someone already has. There are whole classes out there on writing effective communications, and emails are just that – written communications. Here are some tricks and tips to make those communications as effective as possible.

Write an email, not a book

Keep your email messages as short and concise as possible – preferably no more than one page. Most people are too busy to read a long message and will only skim something that's long anyway. This is especially true if you're writing to your manager or a large audience.

I know that sometimes keeping the email short can be tough. You feel like you've got a lot of information to cover. But chances are you're too close to your topic, and you need to step back. Most people reading the message probably don't need quite as much detail as you have to offer.

Try writing the message the way you want, and put it aside without sending it for a few hours. Then come back and re-read it. Chances are during the second pass you'll see a number of places where you can shorten, summarize, or delete.

Summarize the message in the first sentence. Ask "so what?" Then get into the details.

Your first sentence, like your email subject, should focus on summarizing the issue and telling the reader what you need from them or why you're sending them the message.

Write a summary sentence and ask yourself "so what?" Pretend you're the reader, asking the writer this question. Why should the reader care? Answer it, and that is the new summary sentence. Now ask "so what?" again and keep going until you can't dig any deeper.

Know your audience and use appropriate style/language.

Pay attention to the recipient list of your message. And then consider the language, style, and tone of voice with which you write.

If you're writing a message to your manager, you will want to keep the style more formal. You will want to be as clear and articulate as you can, and you will want to show as respectful a tone in the message as you would use when speaking directly to your manager.

If senior management is going to be receiving your message, you will want to take the time to read, rewrite, and re-read the message as many times as it takes to make it perfect. Run the spelling and grammar check tools. Don't worry – you probably don't write these very often, so take the time to get it right the few times you do.

On the other hand, if you're writing to your coworker/buddy who you communicate with daily, you can keep the message style more relaxed and familiar. However, even with a coworker, don't forget basic polite, respectful behavior. Remain professional, and don't forget "please" and "thank you"!

Create single subject messages wherever possible

Try to keep your message to just one topic. If you feel you need to discuss a couple of different topics, write separate emails.

Otherwise it's possible that your reader will only catch on to one topic and miss the other altogether. Also, if there are a few people on the email message and one topic starts an ongoing email conversation, you risk having people included who really don't care or aren't involved in the particular topic that is being expanded on.

Respond to the whole email, not just parts.

If you're responding to someone else's message, make sure you respond to the entire message. Remember, not everyone is the expert written communicator that you soon will be, and other

Step 5. Working at home

messages may be very long, with multiple topics and little guidance on what the author is looking for.

So make sure you read the whole message carefully, and don't miss anything in your reply.

If the message is long, make it easy to scan.

If you absolutely can't avoid a relatively long, detailed message, break it up and make it easy to scan through.

Like a newspaper article, the most important information should be at the top and the details should be lower down. I'll often put little sub-headings on sections of a long email to show which parts of the message are the background info, vs. the problem, resolution, etc. For instance:

Dear Manager,

I need your advice/input on the following issue:

Problem: We have a problem with …

Option 1 (recommended): My recommended option is …

Option 2: The other option is …

Pros and Cons: I recommend Option 1 because …

Background: Some additional background you may not be aware of which affects these options is …

Message Recipients

I realize the message recipient (To/CC/BCC) portion of the email seems like it should be straightforward. But even here, there are some considerations to keep in mind.

TO: and CC:

Here are a few tips for the TO: and CC: fields:

Include anyone who needs to know

Now that you're telecommuting, email will replace the vast majority of your opportunities to communicate with your team, coworkers, etc. You no longer have the convenience of being able to quickly pass some information on to someone as you walk past their desk on the way to your own after visiting the vending machine.

So take advantage of the nature of email to allow you to pass information on to multiple people simultaneously. If you're passing some information on to a teammate about a small change to your project, think about what other teammates and co-workers might want to know about this. Perhaps even your boss should see the message, so he's aware of what's going on.

If in doubt, include

I remember when I was relatively new to the corporate world I wasn't sure how often to CC: my boss on messages I was sending to other teammates. I wanted to keep him informed but wasn't sure what details he would or wouldn't care about.

I asked him for advice, and he gave me some great guidance. He told me to let him decide. In other words, if in doubt, send the message to him, too. If he didn't need to know, he'd delete it. If he felt after a while I was sending him too much, he would let me know.

Well, he never did come back and tell me to send him less email so I guess I must have been doing it right. But I was definitely erring on the side of excess – sending him messages even when I wasn't sure if I should. So I've stuck to this rule and in general have found people would rather get a bit too much from you than too little.

Use CC for people who you want to keep informed

Think about whether you put each recipient on the TO: list or the CC: list. The TO: list is for the people to whom your message is really directed. These are the people you really want make aware of the situation, or need to take action or provide feedback.

The CC: list is more of an FYI (For Your Information). These are the people you don't really expect to reply (unless perhaps they know something you didn't realize), and don't need to take any action. You are just "keeping them in the loop" on the conversation that you are having with the members of the TO: list.

Include anyone who you talk about in the message

Often in an email you end up talking about other people. "Boss, Mike told me that his project is going to be pushed out a month which impacts my project in such-and-such way." Or "Sarah, I hear that Tom is going to be on vacation next week. So let's put off our meeting until the following week, as I really want him there."

Whenever you talk about someone else, make sure you CC: them on the message. If nothing else, this is a courtesy to show them that you're not trying to talk behind their backs.

Even if there's nothing negative about the way you wrote the message, if it falls into the hands of the person being discussed, they could accidentally interpret it negatively (Mike could think if I didn't CC: him that I was blaming him for why my project is late, Tom could think I am upset about how he's timed his vacation). By CC:ing the person it shows to them that you're comments are not intended to be taken in a negative manner.

Step 5. Working at home

Also, CC:ing them gives them the chance to speak up. For instance, perhaps Tom has moved his vacation to a different week since he spoke to you – this gives him the opportunity to tell you not to reschedule your meeting. Or perhaps you misunderstood Mike and his project is only slipping by a week and not a month – now he can correct you and make sure you know your dependent project will not be so badly impacted.

If you do have something negative to say about someone, remember my first rule at the beginning of the chapter – don't put it in writing. Pick up the phone to pass on the complaint or negative feedback. If you put it in writing, there's always the chance that somehow it will fall into the hands of the person you are complaining about!

Don't let the list of recipients get too long

I don't mean to sound contradictory to the item above. There is a fine balance between including a few extra people who you think might need to know something and spamming! Most messages you send should only have a few people on the list. Once in a while, there might be some general information that your whole team needs. But if you find almost all of your emails are addressed to more than two or three people, you might want to dial back a bit.

In general, people get so many emails every day that they don't want to be too flooded with extra information that's really not relevant to them.

But there's another reason from avoiding really long TO: and CC: lists, and that's mail storms. Keep reading for more information on that.

BCC: list

BCC stands for Blind Carbon Copy. It sends a message to someone, but none of the other recipients can see that you sent it. They can see who is on the TO: list and the CC: list but never know if you have included someone on the BCC: list. If they do a Reply All, the reply will not go to the BCC: recipients.

Typically BCC: is used when you want someone to be aware of some information you're sending, but don't want anyone to know you're keeping this person in the loop. It's most often used with sensitive situations.

For example, perhaps you've discussed a mutual concern with a team member. You've decided to bring the concern to your manager. You don't really want to volunteer to him that your team-mate has the same concerns (that's your team-mate's business to decide if he wants to tell your manager), but you do want to let your team-mate know that you sent the message. This is a good opportunity for using BCC:.

Another example is if you're having some difficulty getting someone to deliver a project or item they are responsible for and you need to send them a somewhat strongly worded message to let them know they cannot continue to delay. You may want one of your co-workers to see the message so they know you are handling the problem. But, for the sake of the message recipient, you don't want to embarrass them by publicly including others.

> **Tip:** Use BCC: with caution!

However, I strongly discourage you from using BCC: more than once in a very rare while.

The biggest problem with BCC: is that it's not immediately obvious to the BCC: recipient that they were, in fact, BCC:ed. What I mean to say is, they get an email, and there may be a long list of people on the TO: or CC: list. So they may not notice that they were not publicly included in the message recipients and that you don't want others on the list to know they got a copy.

The risk here is they might have something to add and Reply All to add their two cents. Now everyone will realize not only that the BCC: person was sent the message, but that you BCC:ed that person, intentionally including them behind everyone else's back.

I myself have started to Reply All on an occasional message, only to realize I wasn't on the TO: or CC: list just before I hit "Send."

The best way to avoid this problem is to leave the "hidden recipient" off the email altogether. As soon as you've sent the email, go into your Sent box, find the message and forward it to the other person with a quick note like "I just sent this to our boss. But I wanted to show you what I had written."

This way, they know they are not supposed to have received the message, as far as the other recipients are concerned. And there is no risk of an accidental Reply All.

Email Storms (and how to stop them)

There is, however, one time when using BCC: is actually very valuable.

Have you ever received an email sent to a very large group of people, typically a newsletter or a notification about some change coming up? Then immediately afterwards you start seeing messages from individuals in the group saying things like "Please take me off this list, I don't need to receive these updates." Or "How did I get on this list? This has nothing to do with me."

Then you start seeing replies to those people from others in the list saying "Please don't Reply All and spam the rest of us, just reply to the sender only."

Step 5. Working at home

And then replies to those messages from yet different people saying "To those who Reply All telling others not to Reply All, cut it out – you are half the reason my inbox is so full."

And finally another type of reply from a 4th type of person on the list saying, "I don't understand, why am I getting all these crazy messages from everyone, can someone make this stop?"

You are bang in the center of a full-blown email storm, and there's almost nothing you can do to stop it!

On a message aimed at a large enough group of people, these can get so out of control that they end up clogging up mail servers and even temporarily taking down email systems.

How can we avoid these virtual equivalents of a large shouting match? Here are some ideas:

Don't be the cause

If you receive a message aimed at a large group of people and you have something to say to the sender only, please don't use Reply All! Just use Reply – keep your message just to the person for whom it's intended. Here is the one time that the advice to send to too many rather than too few does not apply. If the sender thinks it's really important for the other recipients to know, leave him or her to send an update to everyone. There might be more than one update and they can consolidate everything in one message.

Don't make the problem worse

Do not be one of those people who sends a "Reply All" complaining about all the people who "Reply All." Even if you've seen a lot of "Reply Alls" from people asking to be removed from the list, let that happen and don't respond to everyone asking them to just send to the sender. Most people who have the inexperience that causes them to "Reply All" in the first place also don't read through all the messages with the same subject before they write their message. So chances are they won't get your message until it's too late.

Plus, those who "Reply All" complaining of others who "Reply All" are really being hypocrites. They are as much of a problem as the original senders. They are actually guiltier because the original senders are normally just too inexperienced to realize the problem they are causing, whereas these guys know exactly what's wrong with using "Reply All."

Use BCC: – prevent the problem from happening

If you are the sender you can make sure an email storm can never happen in the first place. If you are sending a message to a very large group, only put your own name in the TO: list and put all the recipients in the BCC: list. This way no matter what the recipients do, they cannot cause an email storm.

You may want to consider putting some information at the beginning of the message just letting the readers know who the message is going to since they can't see for themselves from the TO:/CC: list. You might say, "This message is being sent to everyone in Bob Smith's organization" or "This message is being sent to everyone who signed up for news about the ABC Project."

This way people who don't think the information is relevant to them know why they were included and, if it's a mistake, can let you know.

Try to nip an email storm in the bud

So, let's say you sent a message and forgot to use BCC: (or figured the group wasn't all that large and the people receiving the message wouldn't cause an email storm). Now you start seeing the storm brew – a few messages that should have come just to you were sent to the whole list.

You don't really want to be just another voice telling people not to "Reply All" and causing people to "Reply All" to you. But as the sender you have a little more control.

You can send another politely worded message to the whole group – this time be sure to use BCC: - apologizing for starting a potential storm and asking everyone to "Reply" only to you to this particular message to prevent the email storm from getting out of control.

Once people see this, they will be more likely to hold their tongues (or fingers) and let the storm blow out. Also for those people who want to get off the list or don't understand why they're seeing all the replies, they will (hopefully) reply to the second message that uses BCC:, so even if they "Reply All," it won't add to the storm.

Tip: If you're not the sender but are in the middle of an email storm, you can politely send this last suggestion to the sender and advise that he or she try this idea.

Email Etiquette

The above sections should be a good start in helping you communicate clearly, effectively, and precisely by email. There are also a few matters of email etiquette to which you should pay attention. Here is a short list of things to be aware of:

Don't use fancy formats/fonts/signatures:

Your recipient may not be able to read these, especially if they are not using the same software as you. Also these fancy fonts and colors add to the size of the message – many people have a maximum amount of storage space and do not look kindly on people filling up that space unnecessarily.

Step 5. Working at home

DON'T TYPE IN ALL CAPITALS

This is the written equivalent of shouting. Even if you do feel like shouting, it's never appropriate.

Don't send an email while you are feeling very emotional

We often later regret what we say when we speak (or write) in anger. If you're upset about a situation, wait a little while to cool down before sending the message.

If you can't wait and the situation is urgent, abandon email altogether and pick up the phone. Even though you'll still be upset, a direct verbal conversation reduces the likelihood of further misunderstandings and has the added advantage that it can't be forwarded on to your boss or others.

Don't discuss personal topics or provide personal information

Remember the number-one rule about not putting anything in writing that you wouldn't want forwarded to a broad audience. Even if you trust the person you're writing to, mistakes can be made, and you don't want your personal information or situations broadcast around the company.

Again, this is what the phone is for.

Don't use a lot of acronyms or technical jargon

This goes back to knowing your audience. If any of the recipients of the message may not understand a particular acronym, spell it out. The same holds for very technical terminology that applies specifically to your technology or industry if the others on the message list are unlikely to be familiar with.

Remember if you've added them to the TO: or CC: list, it's because you think it important for the person to receive the information – so why write something they may not understand?

Don't use 'Reply All' inappropriately

If a message has been sent to a group of people, you may not always need your reply to go to the entire group.

For instance, if someone is sending a regular update or monthly newsletter you may want to ask the sender to remove you from the group. Or perhaps you want to send them a quick thank-you for taking care of a situation, and it's not such a big deal that you want the thanks to be recognized by the whole team. Or maybe you want to comment on a side note of the message that isn't relevant to the other participants.

In these cases, you don't need to flood everyone's inbox with your messages. So use the "Reply" button and not the "Reply All."

Don't use 'Reply' inappropriately

Similarly to the previous item, using "Reply" instead of "Reply All" can also be a mistake. Remember that you're telecommuting emails can often take the place of those group chats that happen between you and a few coworkers in the aisle.

If others are CC:ed on an email that is sent to you and you forget to "Reply All" and simply "Reply" to the sender, those other people do not get to benefit from the wisdom of your response. They drop off the message thread and miss out on any further discussion on the topic.

Use a carefully written signature

A signature is the identifying information at the end of your message. As well as including your name, you should also include relevant information about yourself, where you work, and alternative methods to reach you. For instance:

Jane Doe

Network Engineer

IT Division, ABC Corporation

Phone: (123) 456-7890

Fax: (123) 456-7899

jane.doe@abc-corp.com

http://abc-corp.com

Most email applications allow you to pre-set your signature, so every time you create a new email message it will automatically fill the signature in at the bottom. Saves a lot of typing (and typos)!

Use your out-of-office responder appropriately

Your out-of-office responder is a pre-written message that is sent automatically to anyone who sends you an email. You typically set these up when you're on vacation or for some other reason can't respond to emails for a period of time. It sets the recipient's expectations that they won't be hearing back from you quickly so they know not to wait for you if they have an urgent matter.

This message is even more important when you telecommute. When you're in the office every day, people can see when you're suddenly gone. They are also more likely to have discussed your

Step 5. Working at home

trip with you before you left, so they'll know when you are returning. When you're always out of sight, people may easily forget that you're on vacation – especially if it's just for a day.

Your message should have the following information:

1. When you will return.
2. Whether you will be checking email occasionally or not at all while you're gone.
3. Who to contact for urgent matters in your absence.

The message should be kept brief and written in a professional manner. Here is an example:

Thank you for your message. I am on vacation and will not be returning to work until Monday, June 30. During this time, I will not have any access to email.

If this is an urgent matter please contact my team-mate, Jim Grey, in my absence at jim.grey@abc-corp.com.

I will respond to your message as soon as possible on my return.

Jane Doe

Network Engineer

IT Division, ABC Corporation

Phone: (123) 456-7890

Fax: (123) 456-7899

jane.doe@abc-corp.com

http://abc-corp.com

Reporting Status

Let me switch gears for a moment before I end this chapter. As I said, email is just a tool. The previous sections of this chapter have given you a lot of advice on how to use the tool as effectively as possible. But let me now give you one final technique that helps you use the tool to directly help you improve your virtual presence.

As I said before, to improve your virtual presence and avoid the dreaded out-of-sight-out-of-mind phenomenon, you need to make sure your manager and coworkers know what you're up to on a regular basis. This way they won't gradually assume you're spending your days at home doing the laundry, watching Oprah, and lying out by the pool (although technically, who says you can't take your laptop out in the back yard and soak up some rays while you work?).

www.GovernmentTrainingInc.com

Also, if they know what you're up to, there's more chance for them to realize you might need to be involved in something they're working on due to cross-project interdependencies.

So try writing up a short report each week on what you're working on and emailing it to your boss and your teammates.

Remember – people are busy. Don't get wordy or go into gory detail. Use bullet points to hit the highlights of what's been going on in your projects this last week, get straight to the point and don't take up any more of someone's reading time than you need to.

Now some people may feel reluctant to do this, because they don't want to seem like they're pushing themselves forward or boring others with details they don't want.

People sometimes are so busy they forget how busy their peers are. They forget that their peers are just as guilty as they are of only reading half the emails in their inbox, multitasking and working on other tasks during a corporate presentation, even turning off their brains and taking a mental catnap during the boss's staff meeting.

So realize that your coworkers probably know a lot less about your projects, products, and the work you're doing than you think. If you're telecommuting, this situation is even worse. Sure, sometimes it doesn't matter and, in fact, your coworkers may just delete your status report message immediately. But others will care, will have dependencies with your projects, will read your messages and will appreciate the update.

If you feel awkward you can start the first message with "Now that I'm telecommuting I want to make sure I maintain visibility with my team members and, therefore, will be sending this weekly status message to give you guys insight into what I'm up to."

After that, just send the status by itself each week. Maybe after some time has passed, follow up with a few of your coworkers – ask them if they read your status messages and if so, do they understand what you've written and are the messages helpful? You can start to gather feedback on how clear your messages are, and whether you provide sufficient context and over time improve the quality (while maintaining or reducing the length) of the status messages.

Instant Messaging

There is a cartoon I have seen circulating around in the past with a definition for the comical term "prairie-dogging." It showed a landscape of cubicles, and here and there a few people were popping their heads up above the cubicle walls (like prairie dogs) and looking around - to locate someone in particular or just to see who else was in the office.

Step 5. Working at home

Instant Messaging (also known as IM) is a tool where you can engage in a typed conversation with someone else at a different location. You type in a small window and it immediately displays what you typed on the other person's screen as soon as you hit "Enter."

Instant Messaging is sort of the virtual equivalent of prairie-dogging. It gives you the ability to pop up on someone's screen and get their attention for a quick question or to see if they're available for longer. And it's also a tool for your coworkers to take a peak and see if you're available when they need you.

As with the phone and email, IM is another tool that the non-telecommuter uses frequently. But again, they use it as a secondary method to communicate with their coworkers; most of the time they simply talk to them directly. The telecommuter must rely on IM as a primary mode of communication and therefore has an even greater need than his non-telecommuting peer to use it in a highly effective manner.

Which IM Tool to Use

IM is a very important tool that can reduce the out-of-sight-out-of-mind phenomenon. The first thing you should do when you start telecommuting is add all the members of your team, plus your manager, to your IM list.

If you're lucky, your whole team all uses the same IM program as there are many of these. If not, it's worth trying to convince your boss to get them to consolidate.

It's not just good for you. Even if your teammates are all in the same building, there are times when IM can be helpful for people who sit right next to each other (for instance, if one is on a long phone meeting and the other has a quick question for him).

But if you can't succeed here, don't worry. There are IM "gateway" applications that will allow you to run one program to manage all your IM lists.

Yes, you'll still have to sign up and get accounts on all the IM services your coworkers use (MSN, Yahoo, etc.) but you don't have to run each of these applications individually. Some common IM gateway applications are Gaim and Pidgin.

Using IM Well

Now, let's talk about how to use IM well. Imagine it truly as the virtual replacement to standing up and peaking at your coworker over a cubicle wall. Here's a scenario:

Step 1: Question for your coworker

If you have a question for your coworker, the first thing you do is stand up, look over the wall, and see if he's there. That's the equivalent to looking on your IM list to see if your coworker's status is set to "Available" or "Away."

These status settings are normally pretty accurate. Most of these IM tools automatically change to "Away" when there's a fixed amount of time with inactivity on a person's keyboard/mouse. Then they automatically change back to "Available" when the person types on the keyboard or clicks the mouse button.

Step 2: Asking if your coworker can chat

Next, you ask if they have a minute to chat. If you see they're on the phone sometimes you might even make primitive hand gestures, such as pointing at your watch and mouthing the question "Will you be done soon?" or "Let me know when you're done" at them.

This is equivalent to sending a short IM message asking if your coworker has time to talk.

Step 3: Asking the question

Now, if you have a short question and your coworker is available you'll hang over the wall and have the quick conversation right there. This is the same as asking your question via IM.

However, if you need a longer, more complex exchange of ideas you'll step out of your cubicle and go sit down in your coworker's cube. The virtual equivalent here is to ask, by IM, if you can call the person. If they say yes, pick up the phone and initiate a conversation directly.

IM is also a replacement for the cooler gossip. It's where you send a quick note to your buddies asking if they heard about the latest re-org or who got laid off in the latest round of headcount reductions, etc. It's where you compare notes about your boss or make disparaging comments about the political machine driving your company.

These little chats do help strengthen the relationships on a team and provide opportunities for you to get snapshots into what your teammates are up to.

Tip: Do be a little careful about what you say over IM. Some companies have IM pre-set to store a history of what is typed.

I'm not one to buy into conspiracy theories or corporate management playing Big Brother, and don't think anyone is monitoring your every move. But in general, even while having conversations with your coworker buddies about your frustration with upper management, it's always wise to keep what you say and how you say it at a reasonably professional level.

Step 5. Working at home

In fact, IM goes even further than just being the virtual equivalent of the gossip around the water cooler. In face-to-face situations, you have to *go* to the water cooler to have the gossip. What I mean is you can't say what you want when you want.

Suppose you're in a really dull meeting, and you can hardly stay awake. Or you're lost and confused and have no idea what the speaker is talking about. If you're in a face-to-face meeting there's nothing you can do but suffer quietly and then go compare notes with your teammates, at the water cooler, when the meeting is over.

But with IM, if you're telecommuting you can now send messages to your coworkers during these meetings to see if you're the only one who is lost, confused, bored, etc.

And while these opportunities may not seem very significant, I have found myself in many a critical situation where I used IM to communicate with a coworker in a truly important way. Here are a few examples of ways IM can really help you out in a phone-based meeting:

- ☐ Stop someone from saying something you didn't want revealed during a cross-organizational meeting ("Tom, don't mention quite yet that this is going to be more expensive than we were hoping").
- ☐ Get someone to ask a question that wouldn't be appropriate coming from you ("Hey boss, can you ask them if this feature is really something they need or just a nice-to-have").
- ☐ Check with someone before making a statement or commitment to a larger audience ("Hey John – you need five weeks, not three, to finish writing this code right?").

IM Mistakes

Now you see how vital IM can be in your arsenal of successfully remaining present in someone's mind when you're not physically present. So let's take a minute to talk about a couple of important mistakes that you're going to want to avoid when using IM.

Speaking more publicly than you intended:

Have you ever been at a crowded party where you had to shout just to be heard by the person next to you? Then suddenly one of those rare lulls occurs where almost everyone stops talking at once and you realize the whole room has just heard you tell your buddy how attracted you are to the guy/gal with the nice backside standing by the door!

Well, there is a virtual equivalent of this, related to Instant Messaging.

Imagine you send your teammate a short IM telling him how you don't want to announce this publicly yet, but you think your project might slip out past the deadline and this will have some big impacts to other projects. Only it turns out your teammate is on a phone meeting with your boss and your boss's boss presenting a slide set via a virtual screen-sharing tool that allows them to see everything on his screen. Or maybe your boss is in your coworker's office, chatting with him, and happens to be sitting so he can see the monitor.

Either way - OOPS! Now the cat is really out of the bag!

The lesson to learn here is …

Do not start blindly typing away on IM to someone without first confirming that they are there and that they can respond.

My husband and I have a rule that when one of us wants to IM the other, all we type is the word "hi" and nothing more (not even "hi honey"). Then we wait for the other to respond. If there's no response, it's quite possible there are other folks around who can see the screen (either virtually or directly), and now isn't an appropriate time to chat.

I tend to use that same rule with my coworkers.

I'll just say "Hi". Or "Hi, do you have a minute for a quick IM?" and then nothing more.

If my question or comment is urgent (and especially if it's more than just a few words) I'll start typing the message into the IM window and then just sit and wait (or, because I'm always multi-tasking, go look at email). As soon as they respond, even if it's just with another "Hi," I assume it's safe to dive in and I hit "Send" on my pre-typed message.

If people are in a situation where it's not appropriate for them to chat freely, they'll either ignore you, or send a message that says "Can't talk – later."

Tip: If you have an important presentation that you will be performing virtually, and you will be sharing your computer screen, don't take the chance that a buddy won't IM you with something inappropriate for the meeting participants' eyes. Change your IM settings to Do Not Disturb or something similar. Some settings even block IM messages completely.

Saying too much:

The other mistake I've seen people make isn't quite as critical, but can still be detrimental to your efficiency. And this one is easier to fall into.

Sometimes you'll start out what you expect to be a quick conversation with a coworker via IM. But before you know it, the topic has become much more complex and you're both typing frantically back and forth debating the subject at hand.

At this point it's time to say "Hey, let's finish this by phone – it will be easier. Can I call you?"

IM-ing, even for the fastest typist, is much slower than talking directly. Time is money, and you don't want to waste it when you have plenty of other work to do. Also, if the conversation is

Step 5. Working at home

becoming somewhat heated, picking up the phone can really help. A lot of the subtle nuances of the conversation that you can achieve by phone can be lost in IM. So don't be afraid to suggest a phone call.

While I've seen some guidelines on how many IM exchanges you should have before you stop and suggest a phone call, I find that doesn't work for me. I think everyone has a different level of comfort with IM, plus every conversation is different.

Judge for yourself if this quick question is turning into a deep conversation or if the intensity of the chat session is growing. When you think either of these is occurring, fall back on the old-fashioned phone option!

Communicating Differently

As I said earlier in this book, be prepared that how you communicate is going to change now that you're telecommuting.

I previously told you that we get a lot of information from non-verbal cues, such as facial expression, body-language, etc. But we also get a lot of information from audio cues. Not the words someone speaks, but the emotion that you can hear behind the words. So even when you're talking to someone by phone, you get a lot more information than just the words they say.

With Instant Messaging you really are limited in the information you get from someone. All you see are the words the person types. You may be able to glean a little information from the length of pauses between their messages. A long pause may mean you said something that stumped them, or offended them, but often it could just mean they were interrupted – perhaps by a different person IM-ing them. Clearly, this is a very limited solution. So you must be cautious – both in what you type and how you interpret what you're reading.

When you're typing, be careful of using sarcasm as the other person may not pick up the intent. Emoticons (the little happy faces, sad faces, etc., built into most IM services) are very helpful here.

When I'm making a joke, I normally use the happy face or winking smile to make sure people realize I'm just kidding. Or if I'm saying something that I want to make sure they realize is bad news and I'm not joking, I'll use the sad face. I also use the sad face if the person I'm talking to is complaining or upset about something to show I understand what they're feeling and commiserate with them.

These emoticons can really help tell the reader how you intended them to interpret your words or how you're responding to what they are saying (don't forget, they don't have that audio feedback from you either).

www.GovernmentTrainingInc.com

Similarly, be careful of how you interpret what other people write to you.

Perhaps they are not so careful about how they use IM. If you read something that seems odd to you, ask if they're just kidding or mean it. Or ask if what they're telling you is bad news or good news if it's not clear.

Don't be shy. I know sometimes you might be afraid that they'll judge you for asking stupid questions, but you're probably not the only one who has ever struggled to understand them and you wouldn't be asking the stupid question if they did a better job of expressing themselves in the first place.

In general, it's best to give people the benefit of the doubt over IM – if there are two ways you could interpret something someone said and one of them is insulting or upsetting, assume they meant it the other way. Most people are trying to do a good job and work well with their peers – so don't look for trouble needlessly.

Also, if you find certain people are difficult to IM with because you can't tell how they mean things, make it a point with those people to keep your IM conversations shorter, and pick up the phone to call them sooner than you would with others.

IM is just another tool – when it doesn't help, stop using it!

IM Summary

This chapter has covered a lot of information about IM, so here's a quick summary for you to refer to:

- ☐ Try to get your whole team to consolidate on a single IM application. If that fails, use a gateway IM tool to connect to your team members' different IM applications in one place.
- ☐ Use IM for quick questions, or to exchange a quick private word during a meeting.
- ☐ Check with the person you're IM-ing if they are available to chat by IM before you dive in – you never know who might be looking at their screen.
- ☐ Limit IM conversation lengths – if things get too long suggest you switch to a phone call.
- ☐ Use emoticons to make sure your reader understands the intent of what you say. Avoid sarcasm over IM unless you use emoticons to make yourself clear.
- ☐ Don't assume the worst if the person you're IM-ing with seems to be saying something upsetting or offensive – it's easy to misinterpret what others are saying over the limited communication channel of IM.
- ☐ Minimize IM-ing with specific people if you find it difficult to communicate clearly over IM with them – you do not have to treat everyone equally.

Step 5. Working at home

Group Meetings and Collaboration Tools

Now that you are telecommuting, you will be attending all (or most) of your meetings by phone instead of in person.

If all the attendees of the meeting will be joining the meeting by phone, there are various tools you can use to improve everyone's communications.

Collaboration Tools

Phone Bridge

A phone bridge is the telephonic equivalent of a conference room. A general phone number and an identity number are given to all meeting attendees. They dial into the phone number and a recorded message asks for their ID #. Once provided, they enter a virtual room where they can hear all the others on the phone bridge. This is sort of like three-way calling only with more people.

Depending on what your company has arranged, you may have a number and ID always assigned to you, for your use whenever you need it. Or you may have to set up (probably via a Web site) a phone bridge whenever you need one and you get an ID # associated with that particular scheduled meeting.

If the phone bridge is not always available to you and must be scheduled, make sure you schedule it in advance and set it up with a few more participants than you are inviting (in case someone forwards your meeting invite to someone else). Also set it up to last a little longer than your scheduled time in case the meeting runs long.

Mute Feature on Phone Bridges

When you have many people dialing into a phone bridge there is a very high likelihood that there will be some unwanted background noise.

This could be caused by someone with a bad phone line (or perhaps someone had to call in from their cell phone), and the whole phone call could be overrun with static noise or those distracting echoes that make it so hard to talk.

Or perhaps everyone has a nice quality phone line, but half way through the call a loud and lively conversations starts up right next to where one of the participants is sitting.

This is where the phone bridge's mute feature becomes critical. Typically an attendee can mute their line by pressing a key sequence, such as *1 on their telephone number pad (and a different key sequence, such as *2 to un-mute). Although some people may have a mute button right on their phone, the phone bridge's mute capability is a critical feature for those that don't.

www.GovernmentTrainingInc.com

Tip: When the meeting begins, if there are a lot of attendees and there is any background noise, remind everyone how to use the mute feature of the phone bridge. Be sure you remind them how to un-mute too or they won't be able to join in any conversations.

Web Meeting/Collaboration Tools

Web meeting/collaboration tools allow you to "share" what's visible on your screen with a group of people. This is the virtual equivalent of the projector in the conference room. Everyone accesses a virtual room through their Web browsers, and from there individuals can share their screen or just particular windows of their screen.

These tools often have other features, such as allowing you to IM within the tool, a whiteboard feature that you can draw on and others can see, and some more sophisticated tools that allow you to do things, such as virtually raise your hand to ask a question. Webex is one of the more commonly known tools in this area.

Like the phone bridge, the Web meeting tool is something you normally schedule in advance through a simple Web-based interface, specifying a start time, length, and number of people. Follow the same hints about timing and size that are previously provided for setting up phone bridge sessions.

Running a Group Meeting

If you are the meeting leader, there is a lot you can do to make sure your meeting is successful.

Making it Virtual

Do not feel that if you are the only remote attendee, you need to set up the meeting in a conference room for all the other participants and you plan to call in. There is no reason you can't make it a purely virtual meeting, using a phone bridge and a Web meeting session, and let all participants dial in.

Especially as the meeting leader, it is important you are on a level playing field with all the attendees. By making the meeting completely virtual, it avoids heavy reliance on body language and other visual cues and forces all attendees to be clear and more precise in their communications.

There are also advantages of having a virtual meeting vs. a face-to-face meeting. If the meeting is virtual, people from other sites and locations can attend. People can make it, even if it is at an awkward time for them (they can dial in from their car on their way to another important appointment).

If a question comes up that no-one can answer, you can IM someone not in attendance and get an answer, or even ask them to dial into the meeting for just a few minutes. And that person

Step 5. Working at home

may be able to answer a question via IM, even though they're actually in another virtual meeting simultaneously. Try doing all that with face-to-face meetings!

Meeting Invitation

There are some things you should consider when setting up the meeting and inviting your attendees that will make your virtual meeting go more smoothly:

Include phone-bridge and Web meeting details in the meeting invite.

When you send the meeting invitation to all attendees, pre-schedule your phone bridge and Web meeting sessions and provide the information for these sessions right in the meeting invitation (and while you're at it, include the key sequence the phone bridge uses for muting and un-muting – see the previous section).

This way, everyone has the information they need right there at their fingertips when the meeting starts. The details will not be in an email that is buried somewhere deep down in their inbox around the date you first scheduled the meeting.

If you forget to schedule a phone bridge or Web meeting, and do so later, update the invitation directly rather than sending an email – for the same reason.

Consider time zones

If all your meeting participants are in the same time-zone, this is not an issue. However, if you have meeting participants in other parts of the country or world, keep their time-zone in mind.

If you have attendees in other countries that have drastically different time-zones, you may have to schedule your meeting at the very beginning or very end of the day, so that it is a somewhat reasonable time for them.

In general, if there is just one person in a completely different part of the world, he may be used to taking meetings late in his evening for instance (as a courtesy, try to check with him first). But if the group is well distributed, try your best to make the times manageable for all involved.

If you have coworkers in the same country or continent, but perhaps just an hour or two earlier or later than you, chances are picking a time for the meeting won't be too difficult. The only thing you may want to consider is avoiding the very beginning or end of the day and, if possible, avoiding your participants' lunch times. This is easier if you are only dealing with two time-zones. If you have three or more time-zones, avoiding these times pretty much kills most of the day. If these teams are used to working together, they are probably all used to keeping their lunch hour flexible already.

Once you have chosen your time, make sure it is clear for everyone in every time zone. Your calendar application may automatically convert the meeting time in the invitation for the appropriate time zone of each attendee. However, if you write the meeting time down anywhere in the body of the invitation or in any notes, make sure you list the time zone you are coming from.

Send out the presentation file in the invitation

Even if you are planning to use a Web meeting session to share your presentation slides, it's still not a bad idea to include the presentation file in the meeting invitation.

This will let people get a sneak peek about the topic of the meeting (which may help them prepare better) and provides flexibility if someone is in a crunch and has to take your meeting from their car (they can look at the slides in advance – I am not suggesting they follow along on a printed copy of the slides in heavy traffic!).

Also, if the company network is experiencing outages, or if your own home Internet access is encountering problems, having a copy of your presentation in everyone's hands could just save your meeting.

Maintaining the Focus

Let's face it, we are all overworked these days. We have more things to do than there are hours in the workday, and we are all juggling more balls in the air than ever before.

So when you are attending a virtual meeting via your Web browser and you happen to notice an urgent email pop into your inbox, it's easy to just see what it says and maybe send a quick reply while someone else is talking in the meeting.

And while you're at it, there are a few other emails in your inbox you hadn't noticed – why don't you just take care of them too …

Before you know it the meeting is half over, and you haven't heard a thing that has been said. Or, worse yet, you suddenly hear your name and realize someone is asking you a question and you don't have a clue what was being asked.

As a meeting leader, it is your job to try to keep your attendees' focus on the topic at hand, battling the distraction of their emails, IMs, etc. Here are some techniques you can try:

Request people shut down email, IM at the beginning of the meeting

If this is a very important meeting with some very complex decisions to be made, you can politely point out that you need everyone's undivided attention.

You can remind people that this discussion will take a lot of intense focus and that it might help them to shut down their email and disable their IM for the course of the meeting.

Be sure to keep this polite. No-one appreciates demands. Try to make it sound like it's to their benefit to do this.

Step 5. Working at home

Accept you will lose some people, especially minor players

Of course, we all think our own meetings are critically important and all attendees must drop everything to listen eagerly to every precious word we have to say.

But the truth is, some folks are just there for information – to hear the discussion (or perhaps just the end result of the discussion). Other folks have been dragged to your meeting even though they have little interest in the subject, just in case the conversation requires information that only they can provide.

The temptation to multi-task when you're attending a meeting virtually is too great to resist all the time. Accept some people will tune out.

This is a new way of thinking and operating as compared to a face-to-face meeting where it's very obvious and difficult to start working on some other activity. So the dynamic changes a little.

On the one hand the pessimist can argue that people are missing important information and it makes the entire meeting suffer. On the other hand, though, the optimist can say that this manner of attending meetings only half-focused allows more people to be present more often (in case they are needed) while still allowing them to get other work done.

It is not bad, just different. And if you adjust to thinking this way, your meetings can still be very productive.

Be gracious when someone is caught not listening

Now that you've read the previous item, you will understand that some people won't be paying as much attention and this is OK. That means when someone is asked a question (especially a peripheral player who is not deeply involved in the core of the discussion) they quite likely will respond with "Huh? Uh, what? Sorry, I uh, didn't hear the question."

Everyone knows the person was probably busy on something else and not paying any attention. But, as the meeting leader, it's often up to you to set the tone. You can make a relaxed comment, such as "Oh, no worries Bob. I realize you're probably handling 10 other things at once, let me summarize what we were just discussing and get your quick input."

This will make people feel more at ease in your meetings, and in the future more likely to attend your meetings even if they have a lot of other work on their plates.

Try to engage more participation

Imagine you're at a face-to-face meeting with nothing in front of you but a notepad and pen. The speaker is droning on and on, talking through slide after slide after slide. It's all you can do to stay awake!

www.GovernmentTrainingInc.com

Now imagine the same scenario except you're attending the meeting remotely. Chances are you'll spend the entire time working on something else and when the meeting is over you have no clue what any of the meeting was about.

Don't let this be your meeting!

If you have a lot of information to present, try to find ways to get your attendees involved. Ask for their input on the information. Ask them for confirmation or how it will impact them or their projects. Ask them if they like these ideas or have concerns. Ask if there are any risks or problems you have not captured or addressed. Getting your participants more involved will not only keep them alert, but may also provide you with some valuable input that you may not have otherwise obtained.

Keep your meeting focused and to the point

It is perfectly acceptable to spend the first few minutes of your meeting socializing with your coworkers, catching up on non-work aspects of their lives, or even work-related activities outside of the scope of the meeting.

This is no different to the first few minutes of a face-to-face meeting where people sit around and chat a little. This is an important opportunity for you to grow your relationships with your coworkers and help increase your virtual presence.

But when the chit-chat is over, and the meeting gets underway, get down to business. Determine beforehand what the goals of the meeting are and state these clearly at the beginning of the meeting.

Better yet, create a written agenda with bullet points for the topics you need to cover and send it out in advance. If you need to really keep the meeting focused, pick timeframes for each agenda item so you don't find the meeting time has ended, and you're only halfway through your list of topics.

Monitor the discussions, and if you find your meeting going too far off on a tangent, gently guide the conversation back to the main topic. If the tangential topic is important, add it to a "parking lot" list that can be revisited at another time or in another meeting. This allows people to feel more comfortable letting an important topic be put aside so you can return to the original agenda.

The more you stay on track, the more people will pay attention in your meeting and not get sucked away by the call of their email inbox.

Other Suggestions

Here are a few other tools you can use to help maintain an effective virtual meeting:

Step 5. Working at home

State your name

Especially when the meeting is large or there are people who don't know the other attendees well, it can be very difficult in a virtual meeting to know who is talking. This can cause confusions, miscommunications, and simple awkwardness.

Request that all attendees state their names whenever they have something to say. Of course, use this at your discretion – it can be cumbersome when a few people are chatting back and forth. But when there is one primary presenter and people just speak occasionally to ask a question or make a point, it can be very valuable.

Be prepared that even when you request this, people will forget. So set an example and make sure you state your name whenever you speak – it may help remind others. And if someone doesn't state their name and you think it's important don't be afraid to ask them to identify themselves. Soon people will start to develop the habit.

Record action items

Sometimes in a meeting with a complicated or heated topic, the action items that come out of the discussion can be hard to catch. In a face-to-face meeting, when you state that Bob will take care of finding out that statistic you all need, chances are you'll make eye contact with him and he'll give a subtle non-verbal response to let you know he's got it. Even the other attendees in the room will benefit from that non-verbal exchange – they'll know when it's completed and will move on to the next part of the conversation.

But when you're all on the phone, it's much easier for action items to be missed. Yes, if you're lucky you'll be able to get the extra words in edgewise over the heated debate to make sure Bob acknowledges his ownership of the task. And you should try to do this regardless.

But to be safe, make sure you write down each and every action item with the person's name at the beginning. Highlight action items in the body of the meeting notes or make a separate list at the beginning or end of the notes, so when you send them out to everyone they will easily find their tasks.

Of course, in the next meeting on the same topic, review the action item list you created and get status updates from the action item owners.

Get help taking notes

Sometimes you can simultaneously lead the meeting and take notes on the meeting. However, this can be especially difficult if you are doing a lot of talking (can you talk and type at the same time?) or you're in a Web meeting, sharing a set of slides.

Ask another meeting attendee to take notes for you. This will free you up to focus on the conversation and do your job as the meeting leader.

www.GovernmentTrainingInc.com

Be sure to ask someone who you trust will pay proper attention and can do an effective job of capturing the key points. The last thing you want is to check the notes afterwards and discover important items have been missed!

You are the Only Virtual Attendee

In some cases you will find yourself in a meeting where you are the only (or one of the only) participant attending by phone and everyone else is sitting together in a single conference room. This situation is, unfortunately, the hardest to deal with in many ways.

The Projector and Whiteboard

In many meetings, the meeting leader often uses a projector to talk through a slide presentation, or perhaps uses a whiteboard to write out notes or capture the points from a brainstorming session.

Not being able to see this information will put you at a distinct disadvantage.

However, there are a couple of solutions here that you can use:

Ask the meeting leader to use a Web Meeting/Collaboration tool

See the description of these types of tools in Chapter 9. This will greatly help you if the meeting leader is talking through a set of slides.

If the meeting leader is using a whiteboard, ask them if they wouldn't mind typing their notes on their laptop and hooking that up to the projector so the whole team can continue to see the information and you will not be left out. They can even use the whiteboard feature of the Web meeting tool if it has one.

Ask the meeting leader to send you a copy of the slide presentation and other materials in advance

Perhaps there's no projector in the conference room, and the meeting leader plans to print copies of the slides to distribute to the attendees at the beginning of the meeting. Or perhaps there's a projector, but no network access in the room so Web meeting tools are not an option. The meeting leader may not even know in advance for sure if there's network access in the room.

One option is to just ask the meeting leader to send you a copy of the presentation materials in advance, just in case. However, if there's a lot of material, or you expect interactive note-taking that you want to follow along, get creative.

Try to find out for yourself (you're the one telecommuting, you don't want to ask your team members to do extra work to make it easier for you) in advance whether the room has network

Step 5. Working at home

access. Try asking a local admin, or scope out all the conference rooms one day when you do make it into the office, and write down which ones have network access.

If there is no network access, you might even offer to work with the team's admin yourself to book a new conference room – again, take on whatever work you can do to minimize extra effort from the meeting leader just for your telecommuting situation.

Phone Quality

You are definitely at the mercy of your company's choice of phone systems. Typically the larger the company, the more likely they will have a high-end good quality conference room speaker phone, such as the Polycon models. These phones have quality microphones, active noise canceling, etc., to increase the quality of the phone call.

In such a case, you will (hopefully) be able to hear most of what is spoken. With a low-quality speaker phone, though, you may find yourself missing a lot of what is said. And even with the high-quality systems, you may still not be able to catch everything.

There are a couple of things you can do to help you deal with the situation:

If you know your company uses good speaker phones but there's a continuous buzz during the phone call, ask if the speaker phone is right next to the projector. I've seen this happen many times – the speaker phone is too close to the project, and the fan from the projector drowns out all the voices.

- ☐ Or perhaps there is just one person doing most of the talking, and the speaker is too far from him/her. Again, ask if it can be moved.
- ☐ In general, ask everyone to speak clearly if you're having a hard time hearing and make sure they aren't too far from the speaker phone when they talk (e.g. someone may have their chair pushed back far from the table to stretch out their legs).

While you don't want to ask your team members to go to significant effort to accommodate your teleconferencing, small requests like these are not at all unreasonable.

Body Language

You are at a disadvantage to the rest of your team in that you are the only one not getting all the visual feedback from body language that the others are receiving. Much of the dynamic of how the meeting is being run and how the team members are interacting is driven by that visual feedback.

For instance, if you're in a meeting room you can see if there are lots of people having side conversations while you are trying to talk. In this case, you'll either realize what you have to say may not be particularly relevant, or you may decide to politely draw people's attention back to the meeting and then continue with what you have to say.

Or you can see if the silence that just started after someone made a particularly challenging comment is because everyone is thinking or uncomfortable, confused or bored, etc.

But without this information you are at a distinct disadvantage. The best way to deal with this particular challenge is to ask for help.

> **Remember**
> Before the meeting begins, ask someone who you know is sympathetic to your teleconferencing arrangement to help you. Ask him to bring his laptop into the meeting room and make sure his IM is on. Then, during the meeting he can IM you with little comments about what's going on, whether people are chatting on the side, if people seem confused, etc. You can IM him asking if you're the only one who is lost or overwhelmed on a subject, and he can be your eyes around the room.

This may also help with the other problems previously mentioned. A team member can tell you when the presenter moves to the next slide in a presentation, what he/she is writing on a dry-erase board, or fill you in on any comments that you couldn't quite make out over the background noise on the speaker phone.

If someone (such as the meeting leader) questions why your team-mate is bringing his laptop into the meeting, explain the situation, using all the information I have just provided. Unless this person is hostile towards your telecommuting, he will probably accept the explanation.

Avoid the Problem Altogether

Clearly, with all these problems, it would be much easier if everybody dialed in to an entirely virtual meeting. I do not mean to imply that this way, everyone suffers equally. But rather, some of the problems in the previous sections when most people are in a conference room now no longer apply.

You are unlikely to have a bad-quality phone situation if everyone is using an individual phone and there is no conference room speaker phone in the mix. The meeting leader will plan to make sure their presentation can be shared electronically in some way. And the lack of visual cues for all will force everyone to communicate in a more intentional manner, explicitly saying what they mean instead of relying on people to read it in their facial expressions.

If you feel comfortable, ask the meeting leader if he/she would be willing to try making the meeting virtual. You can offer to setup the phone bridge and Web meeting session (others may not have the ability to set these up if they don't run virtual meetings very often).

If you know there are a few of you who will have to call in (maybe there are attendees in other locations, or multiple telecommuters), try banding together. Explain to the team leader that, since

Step 5. Working at home

there are a number of you who will not be attending in person, it may be easier for the meeting leader to hold the meeting by phone due to the advantages we just discussed.

The worst they can say is no, but at least then you have now opened the door to the types of problems you expect to have. When you now make your specific requests to solve these problems, the meeting leader will more likely understand where you are coming from and be willing to help.

Isolation

While this book so far has discussed many of the physical and logistical challenges to telecommuting, these are not always the hardest problems for most people to solve. Depending on your personality, the lack of people around you can truly be the biggest adjustment you encounter when telecommuting.

In an office environment, you are surrounded by people. Your coworkers sit in the cubicles next to you. You bump into people in the hallways (even if they're mostly strangers if you're in a very big company). You eat lunch with friends you've made through your years at your company.

Even on days where you're working really hard on a project and don't lift your head up from behind your monitor all day, you are still aware of the other people around you. You see people walking by and hear the drone of deep discussions, chit-chat and laughter of your neighboring co-workers.

But when you start working at home things are very different. If you have kids at home (and in-home childcare, of course) then there will probably be some background noises of humanity around you. And chances are when you're ready to stop, take a break and stretch your legs, you can chat with your kids and childcare provider.

But for many, there is not even that. A quiet, empty house day after day may be a godsend for some folks who work best in complete isolation, but for others this can be depressing, and in some ways even distract you from getting your work done (in the same way some people can't sleep in total silence and need some white noise from traffic, the TV, etc.).

But have no fear – all problems have their solutions!

Reducing the Isolation

If you feel you are suffering from a sense of isolation, here are some suggestions for you to try:

Go to a gym

Although a non-telecommuter may enjoy using their home DVDs for a workout, a gym is a great opportunity to kill two birds with one stone for a telecommuter. You need to get your exercise anyway, so do it in a very public place. This will give you the general feeling of being immersed in humanity a couple of times per week, even if it is only for an hour or so each time.

You also may find yourself making friends with the regulars there if you keep to a pretty consistent schedule. And now you can have more meaningful interactions with people than just a passing nod at a stranger or two.

Work at a coffee shop

When was the last time you went to a local coffee shop and didn't see at least one or two people there with their laptops open, coffee in hand, working busily?

This is the new era of working anywhere. Why sit in your empty house working when so many coffee shops have wireless network access available (for free or a minimal charge) to their patrons?

You can sit at the coffee shop, working on your laptop, and watch the hustle and bustle of people go by as you work. Just as at the gym, maybe you'll get to know some of the other regulars there and enjoy frequent interactions. And you'll never be in short supply of caffeine!

Look for a co-working facility in your area

A new phenomenon called Co-working is starting to gain some momentum. It is a movement to share office space in a creative, collaborative, cafe-like atmosphere. Co-working facilities are essentially office spaces for the local community. It does not matter what company you work for – many patrons of these facilities are entrepreneurs and free-lancers.

The facilities provide a shared office environment with desks, chairs, wireless network access and, of course, coffee makers. You can come and do your work, surrounded by other professionals in a multitude of different industries.

The advantage is it's close to your home (you don't have to fight a long commute). And you get to beat the isolation blues of working in an empty house.

Even better, you can talk to other professionals about whatever difficulty you're struggling with at the time. Even if they don't speak your industry's language, many professional challenges are the same regardless of the type of work you do. And sometimes you just need a sympathetic ear to talk out your problem and, before you know it, you've come up with your own answer.

There is a huge range in the cost and level of sophistication of these facilities. Some are grass-roots or not-for-profit services. They may be little more than a large room with desks, wireless network, some dry erase boards, and a kitchenette. You can drop in for free, and put money in a tip jar at your discretion for the general upkeep of the facility.

Step 5. Working at home

Others provide much fancier facilities including conference rooms, mail services, and even childcare. Of course, you pay a lot more for these places! So do some searching online – maybe there's a co-working facility in your neighborhood!

Arrange a weekly walk with a neighbor

Perhaps you have a friend or neighbor near you who works out of their own home. Arrange to meet once or twice per week and take a walk together. Try to make it a fixed schedule (every Tuesday and Thursday at 2:00 pm) or else you'll never stick to it!

This will give you the chance to get some of your weekly exercise done. And you'll get the time to socialize and get that human contact you crave.

Use your communication tools, such as IM

Who says IM is only for your business activities? Find out your friends' IM account names (and if you need it, use one of the IM gateway tools described in the IM chapter of this book).

When you're ready to take a short break, have a quick virtual chat with your friend. It's a nice way to keep in touch, and allows you to keep connected even with friends who may be geographically very distant.

Check with your friends when you first start IM-ing them. Some folks don't like to be interrupted during their work day. You don't want to jeopardize a friendship over this!

> Tip: Don't spend so much time IM-ing with your buddies that you find you're no longer getting any work done. For some people this solution can be a slippery slope, so know yourself and use IM with a little care!

Get a pet

For some people, a cat or dog can be just as good company as humans. Having a cat curled up on your lap while you do your work or having a dog eagerly follow you around the house every time you get up from your desk, can go a long way to replacing the lack of human presence around you.

If you've never had a pet before, try offering to pet-sit for a friend who is going to be out of town for a few days or weeks and try it out. See if you're a cat or a dog person, and if having an animal underfoot is pleasant or just annoying.

Don't forget, pets have feelings too. Don't get a pet if you're just telecommuting for a short while and then will be back to long hours outside the house every week – your pet will get lonely and take it out on your slippers or favorite bed sheets!

Give yourself time to adjust

When each of my kids transitioned from being at home with a nanny to attending a formal daycare facility, the adjustment was probably harder for me than for them. For the first week or two in each case, whenever I needed to stretch my legs I would wander aimlessly around my house feeling lonely and disconnected. I had a deep ache inside from wanting to give my babies hugs or just see how they were doing throughout the day. My house felt depressingly quiet.

But I had telecommuted from an empty house before and knew I enjoyed it just fine. So I hung in there. After a few weeks I got back into my empty-house rhythm again. I would find things to do around the house while taking my breaks, such as watering the plants, throwing in a quick load of laundry, or just sitting outside in the sun for five minutes and listening to the outdoor noises.

I used some of the other techniques previously listed too. And in no time I was enjoying my quiet space again.

So don't give up, saying you hate it after just a day or two. Give it a little time. Try transitioning slowly – you don't have to go from five days in the office to five days in an empty house. Start with just a couple of days and then increase it. No-one says you have to make this adjustment all at once!

Professional Networking

The previous section provides ideas to beat the loneliness blues and find some human contact. But there's another aspect of isolation to consider.

When you are at an office building, surrounded by coworkers and peers, professional networking is quite easy. You talk to your teammates every day and develop good relationships with them. Which means even after they find new jobs at new companies, you can continue to contact them occasionally and keep that network alive.

You can also build your network organically.

You may be walking down the halls and bump into someone you worked with a couple of years ago. This person has moved into a different organization within the company and you have not spoken to him in quite some time. But now you get to re-establish that relationship.

Perhaps you're at the vending machine fighting to make it take your old, worn dollar bill. Someone waiting behind you offers to trade it for one of his crisp, clean bills. You strike up a conversation and find out he is in the department you were considering trying to move into.

As you can see, the physical presence of so many people around you makes networking very easy. But when you spend most of your time alone in your home office, professional networking can too easily get pushed to the back burner.

Step 5. Working at home

Don't let this happen!

> Networking is so important. And most people don't realize this until it is too late. You need to build a strong network now, so later when you need answers, are looking for assistance, or have a crisis, you have people to whom you can turn.

Must Do

Try some of the following ideas to keep your professional network:

Attend regular networking events

Your company may hold networking events with guest speakers. Try to attend these on a regular basis. If not through your own company, you may find others open to all professionals or open to members of a group you can join.

Once/week invite a local teammate to lunch

You can come into the office for lunch or arrange to meet halfway between the office and your home if they are willing. Meet someone different each week. These face-to-face connections will deepen your working relationships.

Try to coordinate a team lunch or movie night once/month.

This will give you the opportunity for some face-to-face time with your whole team. These can be valuable, even if you talk to your teammates frequently by phone, because the face-to-face dynamic can be different.

Join a hobby group

If you are in a large company, chances are they have groups for whatever hobby you can think of: book club, toastmasters, running group, meditation groups, etc. Find one that seems interesting to you and try to come into the office for events.

If you're at a smaller company, find a local community-based group. You will meet plenty of professionals this way too.

Talk to your site administrator

Your site administrators often have their fingers on the pulse of social events at your company. Make friends with them and let them know your interest in what's going on. They know when a group in the office is organizing a birthday party, baby shower, etc.

Your teammates may forget to tell you about some of these events simply because you're not around. Or the events may be advertised by posters in the hallway that you don't see if you're not there. But your admin will know.

Join a volunteer activity

Many large companies have heavy involvement in volunteerism. There may be groups within your company involved in all kinds of different volunteer activities.

And if your company is small, again you can find local community-based volunteer activities where you will likely find other like-minded professionals.

When you meet someone at one of these opportunities with whom you seem to get along and have a connection, don't forget to get their contact information. Invite them out to coffee or lunch and keep in touch with them. Build your relationship to strengthen your network.

I know some of the above suggestions in this and the previous section may make some of you ask "Where will I find the time to do this?" But remember, now you're telecommuting you're probably saving at least 40 minutes or more each day from time you would otherwise have spent on the road. So take just a little of that time for some of these activities – it will be well worth it.

Consider a Mentor

Remember: Have you ever had a mentor in your career before? This is someone who is more advanced in their career than you who can provide you with an opportunity to check-in occasionally, discuss your struggles and challenges, and provide advice and guidance.

A mentor should not be your boss or someone on your team. You want a mentor who has distance and perspective from your immediate situation. And obviously, for telecommuting success, you want a mentor who telecommutes frequently while remaining very successful in his/her career.

This will this give you a chance to meet with someone (perhaps virtually, of course) on a regularly scheduled basis to talk about your struggles and difficulties. Because the conversation is not about the immediate projects that make up your job, the connection will seem less like a work activity and more like a relationship.

This will give you another human connection to help reduce any feelings of isolation. And, of course, it will also give you the opportunity to get direct advice from an experienced telecommuter on how to handle any telecommuting concerns or issues you're worried about.

How to Find a Mentor

There are a number of methods for finding a good mentor:

- ☐ If you can think of someone who meets the above description, approach him or her and ask if they are willing to be an informal mentor. Make sure you spell out your expectations – you want to be clear this is not a major commitment. Remember, this person will not be paid extra to do this, so make sure it does not sound like a burden for them.

Step 5. Working at home

- [ ] See if your company has a mentoring program. Many big corporations offer this (although you may have to poke around a little to find it). Once you've found it, there is probably a process where you can sign up to request a mentor or access a list of people who agree to act as mentors.
- [ ] Pay a professional coach. More and more people these days are using coaches to help them with all aspects of their lives. You can find a coach who specializes in any area that you want to improve, be it professionally or personally. Find a coach who specializes in the area you need focus on, whether that is telecommuting or some other aspect of your career.

Co-Worker Hostility

There is one other issue that can contribute to a sense of isolation when working from home. That is your co-workers' attitudes.

Some of your co-workers may feel jealous that you are telecommuting. For whatever reason, they may not be comfortable telecommuting themselves (perhaps they have not read this book!). Maybe they do not have permission to telecommute. Or perhaps they do not believe that you get real work done when you're telecommuting.

These attitudes may show themselves as resentment, anger, or disrespect. And there is nothing more isolating than feeling you do not have a good working relationship with your team-mates. Although these attitudes are rare, they should be watched for.

If you are lucky you will go through your telecommuting career without any sign of these negative feelings. I believe, as technology continues to improve in the forms of increased network speed to people's houses, etc., telecommuting is becoming more common and these attitudes occur less and less.

But if you do see signs of these negative feelings in your co-workers, hang in there. Be sure to use the tools and techniques in the previous chapters as much as you can to make your co-workers' lives easier. Depending on the reason for the negativity, you may focus on different techniques:

Jealousy because your co-worker has not been able to make telecommuting work for himself

The best solution here is to lead by example. Show him how you make telecommuting work, and perhaps he'll realize that he can do it too. Heck, point him to my Web site (http://avoidgoingtowork.com) so he can buy this book!

Jealousy because your co-worker does not have permission to telecommute

This one is a touchy subject. Perhaps there are some things your co-worker can try to get permission (as described earlier in this book). Or again, leading by example may help. As you show your boss how you are able to telecommute so successfully, your boss may relax the rules for your co-workers too.

If nothing else works, remain sensitive to the situation and try not to put too much emphasis on your telecommuting. Over time your co-worker will accept the situation.

Belief that you aren't really working when you telecommute

This one may either show up as disrespect towards you, or perhaps resentment because your co-workers feel they are going to have to pick up the slack.

In this situation, you should really focus on the techniques given in the previous chapters for improving your virtual presence. Make sure you send weekly status reports to your co-workers as well as your boss, so they can all see what you're accomplishing. And make sure you aren't asking them to make many significant changes to accommodate your telecommuting arrangement (see the section on group meetings).

Eventually your team-mates will see the work you are doing has continued at the same level of quality as before and realize you are still working hard.

Discipline

One of the key requirements to truly telecommute successfully is discipline. Many of the potential telecommuting pitfalls listed at the beginning of this book can be overcome with a little discipline.

There are some people who are just very unfocused and undisciplined, and these people really struggle with some of the telecommuting pitfalls. My husband is one of those people – he is very easily distracted and struggles to be truly productive on the days he works from home.

But even for him (and trust me, chances are you're not as bad as he is!) he still chooses to work at least one day per week from home because of all the up-sides. He simply makes an effort to do it on a day he has a hard deadline (as that is sufficient motivation for him to stay focused). Or he'll work from home on a slow day when he's due for a little bit of a break and can take the time to enjoy breakfast with the kids, or schedule a haircut, for example.

If you think you can muster just a little bit of discipline then you are a good candidate for at least some telecommuting!

Avoiding Distractions at Home

Now that you're working from home, there are very different kinds of distractions from those you were probably used to at the office.

Sure there are fewer people around you to interrupt you or to turn your quick two-minute question into a 20-minute discussion about non-work-related matters. In fact, at home there may not be anyone else in the house at all. But there are many other types of distractions in your home.

Step 5. Working at home

A few minutes lost here and a couple of minutes lost there and before you know it, you've lost a few hours. This may be OK once in a blue moon, but if you're working from home regularly, understanding these distractions and having a plan to deal with them is important.

Is it OK to interrupt my workday with household chores?

Household chores, such as doing the laundry, washing the dishes, or cleaning up in the kitchen are typically something that's hard for many folks to get excited about.

Yet when you're stuck on an important paper where you just can't seem to break through, or about to start a very daunting project where you simply have no idea how to get started, even the most mundane activities can seem like a better way to spend your time.

As you walk through your kitchen to get a snack, you suddenly notice the crumbs on the floor and feel an overwhelming desire to pull out your broom and sweep. And not just that spot, you've been noticing the whole kitchen needs sweeping. And the counters could do with a good wipe-down while you're at it.

Yes, all those little things that need to get done around the house can call you away from your computer. So, should you enforce strict discipline and only perform your household chores after your workday has ended?

Well, that depends.

It depends on your personality and your general level of focus and discipline. Some people will find that when they need to take a mental and physical break from sitting in front of their computer, spending five minutes to start up the next load of laundry is sufficient and then it's back to work again.

However, others will find that once they start, they can't stop. It's not that the housework is so exciting, but that it's a stalling tactic for avoiding getting back to your "real" work. You keep hopping from the next chore to the next and, before you know it, you've got a sparkling clean house and you've lost 2 ½ hours of productive work time.

So only you can answer this question. You can try interspersing some of these chores with your work for a week and see if you have the discipline to keep the distractions under control. If it doesn't work, make yourself a firm no-housework policy.

And yes, I do realize that a few of you reading this are wondering if I'm crazy and thinking no matter how much you want to avoid your "real" work, housework will never seem like a better way to spend your time. To you I say, "Congratulations – you will never have to worry about this problem." Oh yes, and "Hire a housecleaner."

Telework: How to Telecommute Successfully

Is it OK to interrupt my workday with TV watching?

As a general rule to this one I would say "no." Watching TV is much longer than a five-minute stretch break (to say nothing of the fact that you're not actually moving around and stretching when you sit on your couch watching TV). And after one ½ hour show comes the next, and then the next.

In general, most people probably don't have the discipline to incorporate TV watching into their workday at home successfully. The only time I could see it working is if your favorite ½ hour TV show is on at lunch time so you watch while you're taking your lunch break anyway. However, even for that I'd say you'll need to be a naturally disciplined person to be successful!

What about surfing the Internet?

Everyone is guilty of spending a little work time surfing the Internet for personal interests. Perhaps you like to read the local news, follow the new gossip on your favorite movie star, or search for reviews on that new cell phone or kid's bicycle you've been thinking about buying. In fact, I know people who always spend the first 10 minutes of their workday in the office reading CNN online.

Most companies generally accept that their employees will spend a little time on the Internet during work hours. It's only natural for people to take short breaks, and during that time they will work on personal tasks.

However, the one advantage (from a work productivity perspective) of doing this in the office is other people are occasionally walking up and down the aisles (and glancing over your shoulder as they do so). You know after a while people will start to notice if you spend too long on Yahoo!

At home, however, there's so much privacy that you aren't worried about who may be glancing over your shoulder. And you lose that natural guilt-based self-monitoring of your actions. So if you find yourself losing productivity when you work at home because you're spending all your time Internet surfing for personal reasons, watch that discipline!

Tips: Try tracking the amount of time you surf, limiting it to ½ hour per day. Try only doing it at a certain time (while you're eating lunch or first thing in the morning). Or make a rule that you don't do it at all if you're the kind of person who works best under an all-or-nothing kind of discipline strategy.

Where did all these people come from?

There you are, hard at work at home when suddenly the doorbell rings.

It's your neighbor. He knows you're working from home and he stopped by with a quick question about the tree that is between your property and his. However, after you answer the

Step 5. Working at home

question you can't seem to get rid of him. He's retired and has time to kill, and he doesn't seem to realize that you are truly working.

You finally get back to work and then the phone rings. It's your sister. She wanted to remind you not to forget your mother's birthday and was just planning to leave a message on your home phone. She was surprised you answered but now she has you, she wants to discuss the latest fight she had with her/your brother. An hour later after you've finally managed to diffuse the potential family feud, you realize you only have ½ hour left to finish that presentation that you had planned to work on all morning.

Sometimes people don't understand that just because you're working at home does not mean your job is any less important. Some people seem to feel that when you're at a big, corporate office somewhere you're doing big, important things. But when you're home, you're probably just messing around and not really working.

Even for those who do get it, they may feel that if you're at home and they've reached you, it's up to you to cut the conversation – after all, they aren't the ones trying to get work done.

Well actually they are correct. It is up to you to set the limits and make sure you're putting your work first.

If you find yourself caught up in a face-to-face or phone conversation with a neighbor, friend, or family member, stick to the initial reason they contacted you. When that's over, politely mention you're working and ask if you can continue your conversation in the evening. Feel free to bend the truth if you need to – tell them you have a big project due very soon, and if you don't get back to it right away you'll be in trouble. If they truly care about you, they will understand and not want to cause problems for you.

If you find this too difficult (either because you can't bring yourself to cut people short or because you can't remember to watch the clock and you lose track of how long you've been talking), avoid putting yourself in this situation at all.

Let your answering machine pick up the phone call. Don't answer the doorbell. Nobody knows that you're not stuck on an important phone meeting and that's why you're not answering. Treat it as if you actually were working in the office – you wouldn't even know they'd called/stopped by until you got home and found their messages. Return the calls and visits in the evening during your non-work hours.

Work-Life Balance

We all know how hard it can be to keep a good balance between our jobs and our personal lives. Too often we find ourselves working long hours, sucked into some urgent project or issue, and barely get the personal time for ourselves and our families.

Fortunately, telecommuting can give some of this time back. You're no longer spending hours each week sitting in traffic – all that time is given back to you for whatever you choose to do. However, even this isn't always a gain as many people can, if they're not careful, find themselves spending all this extra time (and more) working in their home offices.

When you work from home, the boundary between work and personal life becomes that much weaker and hard to enforce. Just as it's easy to get distracted from work by the household chores, it is also easy to keep working late into the early evening hours. Or to stop and check email right before you go to bed to see if there's anything urgent, and then get sucked in.

Watch Your Start and End Time

Becoming aware of the hours you work can help you manage your work/life balance.

Yes, you may be a salaried employee at a corporate environment where you are expected to put in more than 40 hours/week. But most people know their limits. They know whether they're only willing to work 45 hours/week or if they are motivated to put in 60. This is a very personal decision, dependent on your career goals, home-life situation, what's going on in your job at the moment, and other factors.

> **Remember**
> Once you have a feel for how many hours you typically put in the average work week, plan your schedule around this just as you would if you were going into the office. Determine what time of day you plan to start working and when you plan to stop. This will help you get up and get to work in the morning (and not sleep until noon) and will also stop you from working through dinner.

Keep Track of Breaks

Again, you may not be sticking precisely to a 40 hour/week 9:00 am-5:00 pm schedule. However, keeping track of roughly how long your breaks last will help the easily distracted, as well as the workaholic.

If you're easily distracted you might find your breaks add up to more than your work hours every day! If you start to watch the clock a little, you can see if you have a habit of turning a small break into something much longer.

Similarly, if you're a workaholic, you may find the quiet and lack of interruption at home causes you to work so long and hard that you're actually forgetting to stand up, stretch, eat lunch, etc.

So for either personality type, watching the clock just a little more carefully when you first start working at home can help you start off with some good habits.

Step 5. Working at home

Turn off the Computer

Yes, you read that right. It's very easy at the end of the day, to stay logged into work. And then, as you walk by your office on the way to your bedroom at night you take one more peak at your email. But, before you know, it an hour has passed and you're still at your desk.

Turning off your computer when you're done for the day is a psychological indicator that you really are done. For some people, that simple act can allow them to mentally detach themselves from their work and focus on their home/family life. Plus it removes the temptation to just check on things at work before crawling into bed for the night.

You might even try keeping your office door closed when you're not working. This is another way to mentally leave your work "at work" and help you separate your home experience from your office life.

This can be especially important at the end of the day on Fridays, if you're the type of person who might otherwise end up working on and off all weekend just because it's there.

Tip: If you like to make occasional use of your work computer for weekend activities, such as surfing the Internet or reading personal email, try making sure your work and personal email applications are separate, and then close your work email application.

Conclusion

Telecommuting is a valuable tool for many people. It can increase flexibility, save time, save money and in general improve the quality of your work and life.

However, telecommuting is not as easy as simply staying home in your pajamas each morning. Although for very occasional telecommuting there's not much of an adjustment necessary, for frequent, ongoing telecommuting you simply cannot work exactly the same way you did when you were in the office every day.

When you telecommute, your physical presence must be replaced by a virtual presence. There are many techniques provided in this book to achieve this virtual presence. These techniques allow you to choose to telecommute frequently (or exclusively) without having to let your career suffer. You no longer have to choose between an upward climbing career track and the flexibility and convenience of working at home.

You can have your cake and eat it too!

We hope this book provides you with valuable techniques and tools that you can use every day.

"There is more to telecommuting than many people think. Tele-commuting is an art.

People work hard to succeed and get ahead in their careers. Then they decide they want to start telecommuting.

Without the right techniques and skills, you could be doing damage to your career.

I have had many years to learn the right ways to telecommute over the wrong, what tools and methods to use to succeed, and what habits to cultivate. I have learned enough that I now excel in my career, even while I telecommute.

I have written down everything I have learned, plus lots of information I've taken from many other fellow telecommuters – so you have everything you need to know in one simple, clear, easy-to-follow book.

I hope you find this makes a significant improvement to your telecommuting experience. Welcome to the world of telecommuting!

Nicole Bachelor

Master of Telecommuting Success

APPENDIX

Appendix 1. Countering Management Doubts and Concerns

Some Common Myths and the Reality

Myth - All of my employees will want to telework.

Truth –According to one study, only about 20 percent of employees wish they could telework.

Myth - Telework is a full-time arrangement.

Truth - Most employees only telework one-three days a week.

Myth - Teleworkers are out of sight, out of mind.

Truth - With modern technology, teleworkers share seamless communication with their office and clients, at all times.

Myth - As a manager, how will I know the telework employees are actually working?

Truth - If your employees are communicating with you, and their assignments are completed on schedule, then your employees are working.

Myth - Teleworking is really just a substitute for dependent care.

Truth - Teleworkers have work to complete, and must arrange for dependent care, just as if they were working in the office.

Myth - Teleworking and telemarketing are the same thing.

Truth - Teleworking is working remotely from a main office, while communicating with the workplace via email, phone, fax or modem. Telemarketing is the practice of selling goods or services over the phone.

Some of the Doubts Expressed by Management

Once I allow my employee to telework, I will never see or hear from him/her again.

Chances are you will only be dealing with part-time teleworkers in which employees will work at home or at a telework center one or two days per week. Create an environment where employees feel comfortable contacting you, and consider (especially at the outset) scheduling a daily telephone meeting with your teleworker just to check in on work progress. Let your employees know your expectations for their availability if you need to reach them while they are teleworking. Remember, if at any time you feel that a teleworker is not performing as you expected, you can modify or cancel the agreement.

If I approve one agreement, I will have to let all my employees telework.

No employee is entitled to telework; it is not a universal benefit available just for the asking. Each telework agreement should be treated independently. You should consider the requirements of each job or task and the performance of each employee requesting a telework arrangement. Your decision should be based on the merits of each individual request and on maintaining equitable decision-making regarding telework, not simply on what was approved for someone else.

Telework stands in the way of effective teamwork.

Successful teamwork does not require all team members to be together in the same physical place. Effective work planning and communication strategies can support team efforts across time and space for a variety of job tasks and functions. Team members can work together to establish their own procedures for working together; typically these will include a mix of in-person meeting time, phone calls, conference calls, email, and perhaps other methods of working together without being together 100 percent of the time.

Worker productivity will drop if I am not watching my employees every minute.

Rather than experiencing declines in job performance, many organizations that encourage teleworking show improvements in productivity. At a minimum, you should expect telework to have little, if any, negative impact on productivity; that is, the amount or quality of work completed. Teleworkers should be just as productive working from home as they are in the office, assuming you have made the right decisions about which tasks and employees are best suited for telework. If you experience any reduction in productivity with a teleworker, you should work with him/her to identify the problem and solutions, which may include modification or cancellation of the telework agreement.

Work Planning/Scheduling Requirements

You will likely have to make some adjustments to how your office does business to accommodate telework. When your entire staff is in the office every day, it's easy to schedule impromptu meetings. If you have part-time or full-time teleworkers on staff, however, you may need to plan these meetings in advance and/or arrange for your teleworkers to participate via electronic means (telephone, videoconference, Web conference, etc.). When making work assignments, you may also need to coordinate the assignments with your teleworkers' schedule. Teleworkers need to be flexible to accommodate your scheduling requirements.

Appendix

Proximity in the office doesn't guarantee high effectiveness. Many managers of teleworkers report it is beneficial to have to pay more attention to scheduling meetings in advance, instead of always having the luxury of calling meetings on the spot. The latter are definitely necessary sometimes, but in most cases a bit of planning goes a long way in helping all staff members make the best use of their time.

Proven Benefits

Increase management results: Managers with telework employees often have more efficient employees with higher-performance standards. Managing the results of your telework employees will help you to gauge the success of your program.

Allow for business continuity: Teleworking can be a key component of a business continuity plan in the event of bad weather, a pandemic, or any other crisis that closes the central office location.

Expand the human resource pool: There's an untapped talent pool of qualified potential employees who are unable to drive. Teleworking can alleviate the need for transportation altogether, allowing companies to hire these empowered, independent employees. The result is a telework staff with higher morale, work ethic, and company loyalty.

Real Estate Savings: Telework is also a viable solution in reducing physical office space. Estimates in the private sector indicate that telework can cut corporate real estate costs as much as 90 percent. On the public-sector front, many federal agencies have relinquished their office space in favor of "hoteling" programs that reserve workspace for employees who come into the office. According to the Gartner research firm, while the actual reduction in office space depends on how employees use the space, the rental cost for the floor area, and the slight increase in shared office space for teleworkers, the average reduction is still roughly 130 to 140 square feet per remote user per year. The result is significantly reduced real estate maintenance and cost.

A telework program in Loudoun County, Virginia, recently expanded the traditional definition of telework to include mobile workers. The program provides county building inspectors with the tools to complete their tasks in the field and at home, without traveling to and from the office. The county has equipped building inspectors and supervisors, approximately 70 employees, with notebook computers containing broadband cards and virtual private network (VPN) access to the county's network and its applications. Through the program, each inspector can receive assignments, conduct research, and communicate inspection results remotely, eliminating the twice-daily drives to and from the main office every workday. Loudoun County hopes to realize $95,000 in savings when the current office lease expires.

Continuity of Operations (COOP): Business as Usual

Responsible for initial response and recovery efforts in times of emergency, state and local agencies must continue to provide support to all constituents regardless of the circumstances. To do this, state and local agencies now find it imperative to incorporate telework into continuity of operations (COOP) plans. Information technology research firm Gartner, Inc., reports that agencies that implement teleworking as a primary work format stand the best chance to get their employees back to work as safely and quickly as possible. In addition, they are ideally positioned, via remote access, to move rapidly in the event of a disastrous interruption to operations. Rather than being a "break glass in case of an emergency" situation, telework must be implemented into agencies' standard operating procedures to reap the benefits.

Hennepin County, headquartered in Minneapolis, Minnesota, and serving more than 1.1 million people in 46 communities, is one local government that benefited from proper COOP planning and effective telework policy. Instead of shutting down the county government during the 2008 Republican National Convention, the county relied on its telework policy to maintain a "business as usual" workload. Implemented in 1997, this telework policy avoided what could have been a drastic break in business continuity.

Employee Benefits

Work/Life Balance and Cost Savings

Telework Exchange finds that Americans spend more time commuting each year than on vacation. Telework can change that by reducing time in commuter traffic and offering greater flexibility to manage work/life balance. In Alabama's Department of Transportation, new hires throughout the state can now go to their nearest division office for training, rather than driving three or four hours to the central office in Montgomery. The state of Arizona estimates that its employees who telework drive 5.25 million fewer miles and endure 181,000 fewer hours of stress every year.

Telework can also significantly reduce travel costs, especially considering the fluctuating price of gas. Congestion wastes 2.9 billion gallons of gas in the United States each year, creating a $78-billion annual drain on the economy. Telework Exchange research finds that by teleworking full time, the average commuter can save more than $2,000 a year on gas alone. Telework Exchange offers Telework Value Calculators, available at www.teleworkexchange.com, that tally potential cost savings and environmental benefits associated with telework.

Appendix 2. Teleworking and IT Security

All organizations should have an IT security plan in place and this will impact on how teleworkers operate, what devices they can use, and how they communicate with each other and the head office.

Appendix

A telework security policy can limit the types of client devices that teleworkers are allowed to use for remote access. For example, an organization might permit the use of only organization-owned PCs. Some organizations have tiered levels of access, such as allowing organization-owned PCs to access many resources, teleworker-owned PCs to access a limited set of resources, and consumer devices and third-party PCs to access only one or two resources, such as Web-based email. This allows an organization to limit the risk by permitting the most-controlled devices to have the most access and the least-controlled devices to have minimal access.

Each organization should make its own risk-based decisions about what levels of remote access should be permitted from which types of devices. Factors to consider when setting telework security policy include the following:

- **Sensitivity of telework:** Certain types of telework involve access to sensitive information or resources. Organizations with more restrictive requirements for telework involving sensitive information may permit the use of only organization-controlled telework devices.

- **The level of confidence in security policy compliance:** Meeting many of an organization's security requirements can typically be ensured only if the organization controls the configuration of the telework devices. For personally owned devices, some requirements can be verified by automated security health checks conducted by a remote access server, but other requirements cannot be verified by automated means. Making users aware of their responsibilities can help improve security on personally owned telework devices, but will not result in the same degree of security policy compliance as mandatory security controls on organization-controlled telework devices. Even the most conscientious users may fail to properly maintain the security of their personally owned devices because of the technical complexity, the effort involved, or their lack of awareness of new threats.

- **Cost:** Costs associated with telework devices vary based on policy decisions. The primary direct cost is issuing the devices and client software to teleworkers. Indirect costs include maintenance and providing technical support for teleworkers. Another consideration related to cost is telework frequency and duration; an organization might justify purchasing telework devices for regular or part-time teleworkers (e.g., one day per week from home, frequent business travel). However, costs are not justified under certain situations, such as when office-based individuals want to quickly check email from home a few evenings a month.

- **Telework location:** Risks will generally be lower for devices used only in the home environment than for those in a variety of other locations. Also, in some cases the organization can automatically determine the teleworker's location (i.e., identify whether the device is on an authorized home network), making it easy to enforce location-based policies.

- **Technical limitations:** Certain types of devices may be required for particular telework needs, such as running specialized programs. Also, if an organization has a single type of remote access server, and that server can only allow connections through a custom client, then only the types of devices that can support the client are allowed.

- **Compliance with mandates and other policies:** Organizations may need to comply with telework-related requirements from mandates and other sources, such as a federal department issuing policy requirements to its member agencies. An example of a possible requirement is restrictions on performing telework in foreign countries that have strong known threats against federal agency systems.
  - Organizations may choose to specify additional security requirements tied to factors, such as the sensitivity of telework. Many organizations require more stringent security controls for high-risk situations. Helpful security requirements for telework may include the following:
- Permit high-risk telework only from organization-issued and secured telework devices.
- Require the use of multi-factor authentication for access to the telework device and to remote access solutions.
- **Use storage encryption on the telework device to protect all sensitive information.** Multiple levels of encryption may be needed. For example, full disk encryption may prevent an attacker who gains physical access to the device; at the same time, virtual disk encryption or file/folder encryption may stop an attacker who gains logical access to the device (i.e., access after full disk encryption authentication has occurred and the data on the hard drive is being decrypted automatically). Removable media containing telework data should also be encrypted.
- Migrate high-risk resources to secure servers that allow the telework access.
- **Store and access only minimum necessary data.** Some organizations issue "loaner" devices that are completely wiped before and after performance of high-risk telework. Only the data and authorized applications needed for the telework are loaded onto the loaner device. The pre-use wiping ensures that the device is clean before any telework is conducted, and the post-use wiping ensures that no telework data remains that could be accessed in the future. In high-risk situations, organizations may also choose to reduce risk by prohibiting telework and remote access involving particular types of data, such as highly sensitive personally identifiable information (PII).

Every year, there are many changes in telework device capabilities, the security controls available to organizations, the types of threats made to different types of devices, and so on. Therefore, organizations should periodically reassess their policies regarding telework devices, and consider changing which types of client devices are permitted and what levels of access should be granted. Organizations should also be aware of the emergence of new types of remote access solutions and of major changes to existing technologies, and ensure that the organization's policies are updated accordingly.

Appendix

Vulnerabilities, Threats, and Security Controls

All of the components of telework and remote access solutions, including client devices, remote access servers, and internal servers accessed through remote access, should be secured against a variety of threats. General security recommendations for any IT technology are provided in NIST Special Publication (SP) 800-53, Recommended Security Controls for Federal Information Systems. Specific recommendations for securing telework and remote access technologies are presented in this publication and are intended to supplement the controls specified in SP 800-53.

Telework and remote access technologies often need additional protection because their nature generally places them at higher exposure to external threats than technologies only accessed from inside the organization. Before designing and deploying telework and remote access solutions, organizations should develop system threat models for the remote access servers and the resources that are accessed through remote access. Threat modeling involves identifying resources of interest and the feasible threats, vulnerabilities, and security controls related to these resources, then quantifying the likelihood of successful attacks and their impacts, and finally analyzing this information to determine where security controls need to be improved or added. Threat modeling helps organizations identify security requirements and design the remote access solution to incorporate the controls needed to meet the security requirements. Major security concerns for these technologies that would be included in most telework threat models are:

- **Lack of Physical Security Controls:** Telework client devices are used in a variety of locations outside the organization's control, such as employees' homes, coffee shops, hotels, and conferences. The mobile nature of these devices makes them likely to be lost or stolen, which places the data at increased risk of compromise. When planning telework security policies and controls, organizations should assume that client devices will be acquired by malicious parties who will attempt to recover sensitive data. The primary preventative strategies are either to encrypt the client device's storage so that sensitive data cannot be recovered by unauthorized parties, or not to store sensitive data on client devices. Even if a client device is always in the possession of its owner, there are other physical security risks, such as an attacker looking over a teleworker's shoulder at a coffee shop and viewing sensitive data on the screen.

- **Unsecured Networks:** Because nearly all remote access occurs over the Internet, organizations normally have no control over the security of the external networks used by telework clients. Communications systems used for remote access include telephone and Digital Subscriber Line (DSL) modems, broadband networks, such as cable, and wireless mechanisms, such as IEEE 802.11, WiMAX, and cellular networks. These communications systems are susceptible to eavesdropping, which places sensitive information transmitted during remote access at risk of compromise. Man-in-the-middle (MITM) attacks may also be performed to intercept and modify communications. Organizations should plan their remote access security on the assumption that the networks between the telework client device and the organization, including teleworkers' home networks, cannot be trusted. Risk from use of unsecured networks can be mitigated, but not eliminated, by using encryption technologies to protect the confidentiality and integrity of communications, as well as using mutual authentication mechanisms to verify the identities of both endpoints.

- ☐ **Infected Devices on Internal Networks:** Telework client devices, particularly laptops, are often used on external networks and then brought into the organization and attached directly to the organization's internal networks. Also, an attacker with physical access to a client device may install malware on the device to gather data from it and from networks and systems to which it connects. A client device infected with malware may spread throughout the organization once it is connected to the internal network. Organizations should assume that client devices will become infected and plan their security controls accordingly. In addition to using appropriate anti-malware technologies, such as anti-malware software on client devices, organizations should consider the use of network access control (NAC) solutions that verify the security posture of a client device. Organizations should also consider using a separate network for telework client devices, instead of permitting them to directly connect to the internal network.

- ☐ **External Access to Internal Resources:** Remote access provides external hosts with access to internal resources, such as servers. If these internal resources were not previously accessible from external networks, making them available via remote access will expose them to new threats, particularly from untrusted client devices and networks. Each form of remote access that can be used to access an internal resource increases the risk of that resource being compromised. Organizations should carefully consider the balance between providing remote access to additional resources and the potential impact of a compromise of those resources. They should also ensure that any internal resources they choose to make available through remote access, block external threats and that access to the resources is limited to the minimum necessary through firewalling and other control mechanisms.

Protecting Devices

- ☐ To support confidentiality, integrity, and availability, all of the components of telework and remote access solutions, including client devices, remote access servers, and internal servers accessed through remote access should be secured against a variety of threats.

- ☐ Before designing and deploying telework and remote access solutions, organizations should develop system threat models for the remote access servers and the resources accessed through remote access.

- ☐ When planning telework security policies and controls, organizations should assume that client devices will be acquired by malicious parties who will attempt to recover sensitive data from the devices.

Appendix

- ☐ Organizations should plan their remote access security on the assumption that the networks between the telework client device and the organization, including teleworkers' home networks, cannot be trusted.
- ☐ Organizations should assume that client devices will become infected with malware and plan their security controls accordingly.
- ☐ Organizations should carefully consider the balance between the benefits of providing remote access to additional resources and the potential impact of a compromise of those resources. Any internal resources made available through remote access should be hardened against external threats; access to the resources should be limited through firewalling and other access control mechanisms.
- ☐ When planning a remote access solution, organizations should carefully consider the security implications of the remote access methods in the four categories – tunneling, portals, remote desktop access, and direct application access – in addition to how well each method may meet operational requirements.

Ensure that remote access servers are secured effectively and are configured to enforce telework security policies.

Remote access servers provide a way for external hosts to gain access to internal resources, so their security is particularly important. In addition to permitting unauthorized access to resources, a compromised server could be used to eavesdrop on and manipulate remote access communications, as well as to provide a "jumping off" point for attacking other hosts within the organization. Organizations need to ensure that remote access servers are kept fully patched and that they can only be managed from trusted hosts by authorized administrators. Organizations should also carefully consider the network placement of remote access servers; in most cases, a server should be placed so that it acts as a single point of entry to the network and enforces the telework security policy.

Secure telework client devices against common threats and maintain their security.

Many threats to telework client devices include malware and device loss or theft. Generally, telework client devices should include all the local security controls used in the organization's secure configuration baseline for its non-telework client devices. Examples are applying operating system and application updates promptly, disabling unneeded services, and using anti-malware software and a personal firewall. However, because telework devices are generally at greater risk in external environments, additional security controls are recommended, such as encrypting sensitive data stored on the devices and adjusting existing security controls. For example, if a personal firewall on a telework client device has a single policy for all environments, then it is likely to be too restrictive in some situations and not restrictive enough in others. Whenever possible, organizations should use personal firewalls capable of supporting multiple policies and configure the firewalls properly for both the enterprise and an external environment.

Organizations should ensure that all types of telework client devices are secured, including PCs, cell phones, and PDAs. For PCs, this includes physical security (for example, using cable locks to deter theft). For devices other than PCs, security capabilities and the appropriate security actions vary widely by device type and specific products, so organizations should provide guidance to device administrators and users responsible for securing telework consumer devices.

Telework Client Device Security

Telework client devices can be divided into two general categories:

- Personal computers (PC), desktop and laptop computers running standard PC operating systems (OS), such as Windows 7, Vista, and XP; Linux/Unix; and Mac OS X.
- Consumer devices, which are small, usually mobile computers. Examples of consumer devices are networking-capable PDAs, cell phones, and video game systems. Consumer devices are most often used for Web-based remote access, such as portals or direct access to applications, but consumer devices are increasingly supporting other forms of remote access, as well. Consumer devices are often owned by individuals, but some types of devices are frequently owned and distributed by organizations.

The gap between PCs and consumer devices is closing. Some current consumer devices run standard PC operating systems, but these are often not intended for users to direct access. Also, consumer devices are increasingly offering more functionality previously provided only by PCs.

Another set of categories is the party responsible for the security of the client device. These categories are as follows:

- **Organization:** Client devices in this category are usually acquired, configured, and managed by the organization. These devices can be used for any of the organization's remote access methods.
- **Teleworker:** These client devices are owned by the teleworker, who is ultimately responsible for securing them and maintaining their security. These devices are usually capable of using many or all of the organization's remote access methods, if permitted.
- **Third party:** These client devices are owned, configured, and secured by third parties, such as kiosk computers at hotels, and PCs or consumer devices owned by friends and family. Remote access options for third-party-secured devices are typically quite limited because users cannot or should not install software onto them, and even advanced teleworkers cannot force most third-party devices to implement even rudimentary security precautions.

Appendix

In today's computing environment, there are many threats to telework client devices. These threats are posed by people with different motivations, including causing mischief and disruption, and committing identity theft and other forms of fraud. The primary threat against most telework client devices is malware, including viruses, worms, malicious mobile code, Trojan horses, rootkits, and spyware. Malware threats can infect client devices through email, Web sites, file-downloads and file sharing, peer-to-peer software, and instant messaging. The use of unauthorized removable media, such as flash drives, is an increasingly common transmission mechanism for malware. Another common threat is loss or theft of the device. Someone with physical access to a device has many options for attempting to view or copy the information. An attacker with physical access can also add malware that gives them access to data accessed from or entered into the device, such as users' passwords.

Permitting teleworkers to remotely access an organization's computing resources gives attackers additional opportunities to breach security. When a client device uses remote access, it is essentially an extension of the organization's own network. If the device is not secured properly, it poses additional risk not only to the information that the teleworker accesses, but also to the organization's other systems and networks. Therefore, telework client devices should be secured properly and maintained regularly.

Generally, telework client devices should have the same local security controls as other client devices in the enterprise – OS and application security updates applied promptly, unneeded services disabled, anti-malware software and a personal firewall enabled and kept up-to-date, etc. However, because of the threats that client devices face in external environments, additional security controls are recommended; some security controls may need to be adjusted to work effectively in telework environments. For example, storing sensitive data on a desktop computer housed at an organization's headquarters has different ramifications from storing the same data on a laptop used at several external locations.

Organizations should be responsible for securing their own telework client devices and should also require their users to implement and maintain appropriate, often similar, levels of security for personally owned client devices. The mechanisms for securing organization-owned and personally owned telework client devices are similar, but some of the security controls might not be feasible for teleworkers to implement on their own. See NIST SP 800-114, User's Guide to Securing External Devices for Telework and Remote Access, for recommendations for users securing their own telework client devices.

Other security measures particularly important for telework include the following:

☐ Have a separate user account with limited privileges for each person using the telework PC. Teleworkers should use their limited-privilege accounts for regular work and use a separate administrative account only for tasks that require administrator-level access, such as some software updates. This reduces the likelihood of an attacker gaining administrator-level access to the PC.

- ☐ Enforce session locking, which prevents access to the PC after it has been idle for a period of time (such as 15 minutes) or permits the user to lock a session upon demand. After a session is locked, access to the PC can only be restored through authentication. Session locking is often part of screen-saver software. This prevents an attacker within physical proximity of a PC from easily gaining access to the current session. However, it does not thwart an attacker who steals a PC or has access to it for an extended period of time; session locking can be circumvented through various techniques.
- ☐ Physically secure telework PCs by using cable locks or other deterrents to theft. This is most important for telework PCs in untrusted external environments, but is relevant for any environment, including home offices.

If teleworkers work from personal PCs, organizations might want to consider additional security controls. For example, some solutions provide a bootable OS on read-only removable media with pre-configured remote access client software. A user can insert this media into a PC and reboot the computer; this bypasses the PC's OS, which may be compromised, and loads the known-good OS and remote access client software from the removable media.

Another option is to provide teleworkers with specifically configured flash drives. These drives hold organization-approved applications that are executed from a read-only portion of the drives, which protects them from unauthorized modification. Temporary files are stored in another portion of the flash drives, which reduces the likelihood of data leakage onto the PC.

Protecting Data

Telework usually involves creating and editing work-related information, such as email, word processing documents, and spreadsheets. Because that data is important, it should be treated like other important assets of the organization. Organizations can protect data by securing it on the telework device and periodically backing it up at a location controlled by the organization. Organizations can also choose not to allow the organization's information to be stored on telework devices, but, instead, to store it centrally at the agency.

Sensitive information, such as certain types of personally identifiable information (PII) (e.g., personnel records, medical records, financial records), that is stored on or sent to or from telework devices should also be protected. For example, teleworkers often forget that sensitive information on a zip drive used with their device, or printing the information on a public printer, can also expose the information. An unauthorized release of sensitive or personal information could damage the public's trust in an organization, jeopardize the organization's mission, or harm individuals.

Appendix

Encrypting Data

All telework devices, regardless of their size or location, can be stolen. Some thieves may want to read the contents of the data on the device, and use it for criminal purposes. To prevent this, an organization should have a policy of encrypting all sensitive data when at rest on the device and on removable media. There are many methods for protecting data at rest, and they mostly depend on the type of device or removable media that is being protected. Some operating systems have their own data encryption mechanisms, and there are also numerous third-party applications that provide similar capabilities. See NIST SP 800-111, Guide to Storage Encryption Technologies for End User Devices, for more information on encrypting storage on client devices and removable media. Generally, when technologies, such as full disk encryption, are being used to protect data at rest, teleworkers should shut down their telework devices instead of placing them into sleep mode when they are finished with the work session. This helps ensure protection by the storage encryption technology.

Using Virtual Machines

If an organization has direct control over a telework device, the organization can enforce its policies for remote access, updating, etc. For other telework devices, such as PCs personally owned by teleworkers, the organization has a limited ability to enforce security policies. A method for controlling the teleworker's environment is to run a virtual machine (VM) on the telework PC. A user runs a VM image in the virtual machine environment; this image acts just like a full computer with an operating system and application software.

The organization distributes a VM image configured to be fully compliant with all relevant security policies. The teleworker then runs the VM image on the telework computer. When the image needs to be updated, the organization distributes a new image. Using a VM to support telework security works well, as long as the computer itself does not have any malware.

Organizations should consider encrypting all VM images used for telework to reduce the risk of compromise. This can be accomplished through the use of full disk encryption, file encryption, or other means. For high-risk situations, particularly involving access to highly sensitive information, organizations should encrypt each individual VM image used for telework and may also want to provide a second layer of protection through full disk encryption.

Backing-up Data

Most organizations have policies for backing-up data on a regular basis. Such a backup policy should cover data on telework PCs and, if relevant and feasible, consumer devices. However, the policy may need different provisions for backups performed at the organization's facilities versus external locations. If the data to be backed up contains sensitive or confidential information, additional security precautions must be taken, particularly at external locations.

If data is being backed up remotely – from the telework device to a system at the organization – then the communications carrying that data should be encrypted and have their integrity verified. If data is being backed up locally – to removable media, such as CD-R disks or USB flash drives, for example – the backup should be protected at least as well as the original data. For example, if the original data is encrypted, then the data in the backup also should be encrypted. If the original data is encrypted in a portable form, such as through virtual disk encryption or an encrypted VM image, then it may be sufficient to copy that encrypted entity onto the backup media. However, for non-portable forms of storage encryption, such as full disk encryption, the data would need to be decrypted on the telework device and then encrypted for storage on the backup media.

Appendix 3. Remote Access Methods

Organizations have many options for providing remote access to their computing resources. Methods most commonly used for teleworkers have been divided into four categories – tunneling, portals, remote desktop access, and direct application access. The remote access methods in all four categories have some features in common:

- ☐ They are all dependent on the physical security of the client devices.
- ☐ They can use multiple types of server and user authentication mechanisms. This flexibility allows some remote access methods to work with an organization's existing authentication mechanisms, such as passwords or certificates. Some remote access methods have standardized authentication mechanisms, while others use implementation-specific mechanisms.
- ☐ They can use cryptography to protect the data flowing between the telework client device and the organization from being viewed by others. This cryptographic protection is inherent in virtual private networks (VPNs) and cryptographic tunneling, and it is an option in most remote desktop access and direct application access systems.
- ☐ They can allow teleworkers to store data on their client devices. For example, most tunnel, portal, and remote desktop access systems offer features for copying files from computers inside the organization to the teleworker's client device. This allows the teleworker to work with the data locally, such as in a locally installed word processor. Some applications that can be reached through direct application access also allow transmitting files to the teleworker. Data may also be stored on client devices inadvertently, such as through operating system page files or Web browser caches. All data sent to the teleworker through remote access must be covered by the organization's data distribution and retention policies.

When planning a remote access solution, organizations should carefully consider the security implications methods in each category, in addition to how well each method may meet operational requirements.

Appendix

Tunneling

Many remote access methods offer a secure communications tunnel through which information can be transmitted between networks, including public networks, such as the Internet. Tunnels are typically established through virtual private network (VPN) technologies. Once a VPN tunnel has been established between a teleworker's client device and the organization's VPN gateway, the teleworker can access many of the organization's computing resources through the tunnel. To use a VPN, users must either have the appropriate VPN software on their client devices or be on a network that has a VPN gateway system on it. The VPN gateway can take care of user authentication, access control (at the host, service, and application levels), and other security functions for teleworkers.

Tunnels use cryptography to protect the confidentiality and integrity of the transmitted information between the client device and the VPN gateway. Tunnels can also authenticate users, provide access control (such as restricting which protocols may be transmitted or which internal hosts may be reached through remote access), and perform other security functions. However, although remote access methods based on tunneling protect the communications between the client device and the VPN gateway, they do not provide any protection for the communications between the VPN gateway and internal resources. Also, in tunneling solutions, the application client software and data at rest resides on the client device, so they are not protected by the tunneling solution and should be protected by other means.

The types of VPNs most commonly used for teleworkers are Internet Protocol Security (IPsec) and Secure Sockets Layer (SSL) tunnels. Tunneling may also be achieved by using Secure Shell (SSH), although this is less commonly used and is often considered more difficult to configure and maintain than IPsec or SSL tunnel VPNs.

The VPN gateway can control access to the parts of the network and the types of access that the teleworker gets after authentication. For example, a VPN might allow a user only to have access to one subnet, or only to run particular applications on certain servers on the protected network. In this way, even though the cryptographic tunnel ends at the VPN gateway, the gateway can add additional routing to the teleworker's traffic to allow access only to some parts of the internal network.

VPNs are usually established and managed by VPN gateway devices owned and managed by the organization being protected. In some cases, organizations outsource their VPNs to trusted third parties. Such a third party might simply manage the VPN gateway that is owned by the organization, but other third parties offer services where they own and control the VPN gateway. In the latter case, the organization should evaluate the security of the proposed solution and ensure it will support the organization's security policy.

Application Portals

Another category of remote access solutions involves portals. A portal is a server that offers access to one or more applications through a single centralized interface. A teleworker uses a portal client on a telework client device to access the portal. Most portals are Web based – for them, the portal client is a regular Web browser. The application client software is installed on the portal server, and it communicates with application server software on servers within the organization. The portal server communicates securely with the portal client as needed; the exact nature of this depends on the type of portal solution in use.

In terms of security, portals have most of the same characteristics as tunnels: portals protect information between client devices and the portal, and they can provide authentication, access control, and other security services. However, there is an important difference between tunnels and portals – the location of the application client software and associated data.

In a tunnel, the software and data are on the client device; in a portal, they are on the portal server. A portal server will transfer data to the client device as rendered desktop screen images or Web pages, but data is typically stored on the client device much more temporarily than data for a tunneled solution. (However, portals can be configured to allow clients to download content from the portal and store it on the client device or other locations outside the secure remote access environment.) Having the application client software centralized gives an organization more control over how the software and data is secured, as opposed to more distributed remote access solutions. Portals limit the access a teleworker has to particular application clients running on the portal itself. Those applications further limit the access the teleworker has to the servers inside the network.

There are a few types of portal solutions commonly used for remote access. A Web-based portal provides a user with access to multiple Web-based applications from a single portal Web site. An SSL portal VPN is a common form of Web-based portal. Another type of portal solution is terminal server access, which gives each teleworker access to a separate standardized virtual desktop. The terminal server simulates the look and feel of a desktop operating system and provides access to applications. Terminal server access requires the teleworker either to install a special terminal server client application on the client device or to use a Web-based interface, often with browser plug-in or other additional software provided by the organization. Another similar remote access method, called virtual desktop access, involves the user connecting to a system that contains virtual images of standardized, non-simulated operating systems and desktops. When the teleworker is finished with a remote access session, the virtual image is discarded so that the next user will have a clean virtual desktop.

The mechanism for providing an interface to the teleworker varies among portals. For example, terminal server access and virtual desktop access present a standardized virtual desktop to the teleworker, while SSL portal VPNs present each application through a Web page. The nature of

Appendix

this interface is important because it relates to the storage of data, temporary or permanent. For many portals the user interface is virtual, and after the user session is over that instance of the interface is essentially destroyed and a clean version used for the next session. Some portals, such as SSL portal VPNs, can be configured to establish a secure virtual machine on the client device, restrict all remote access data to reside within that virtual machine, and then securely destroy the virtual machine instance and all the data that existed within it when the session ends. This helps to ensure that sensitive information does not inadvertently become stored on a telework client device, where it could possibly be recovered by a future compromise.

Remote Desktop Access

A remote desktop access solution gives a teleworker the ability to remotely control a particular desktop computer at the organization, most often the user's own computer at the organization's office, from a telework client device. The teleworker has keyboard and mouse control over the remote computer and sees that computer's screen on the local telework client device's screen. Remote desktop access allows the user to access all of the applications, data, and other resources that are normally available from their computer in the office. A remote desktop access client program or Web browser plug-in is installed on each telework client device, and it connects directly with the teleworker's corresponding internal workstation on the organization's internal network.

There are two major styles of remote desktop access: direct between the telework client and the internal workstation; and indirect through a trusted intermediate system. However, direct access is often not possible because it is prevented by many firewalls. For example, if the internal workstation is behind a firewall performing network address translation (NAT), the telework client device cannot initiate contact with the internal workstation unless either the NAT allows such contact or the internal workstation initiates communications with the external telework client device (e.g., periodically checking with the client device to see if it wants to connect).

Indirect remote desktop access is performed through an intermediate server. This server is sometimes part of the organization's firewall, but is more often run by a trusted commercial or free third-party service outside the organization's network perimeter. Usually there are separate connections between the telework client device and the service provider, and between the service provider and the internal workstation, with the intermediate server handling the unencrypted communications between the separate connections. The security of this intermediate server is very important, because it is responsible for properly authenticating teleworkers and preventing unencrypted traffic from being accessed by unauthorized parties. Also, if the organization's security policy requires particular kinds of authentication, such as the two-factor authentication required by federal agencies, the intermediate server should support this authentication in both directions.

Before implementing an indirect remote desktop access solution, an organization should evaluate the security provided by the service provider, especially possible threats involving the intermediate server and the potential impact of those threats. The organization can then identify compensating controls to mitigate the threats, such as applying a second level of communications encryption at the application layer, and determine under what circumstances the intermediate system may be used, such as for low-risk activities.

The remote desktop access software protects the confidentiality and integrity of the remote access communications and also authenticates the user to ensure that no one else connects to the internal workstation. However, because this involves end-to-end encryption of the communications across the organization's perimeter, the contents of the communication are hidden from the network security controls at the perimeter, such as firewalls and intrusion detection systems. For many organizations, the increased risk caused by this is not worth the benefits, and direct connections from external client devices to internal workstations are prohibited.

Another serious security issue with remote desktop access software is that it is decentralized; instead of the organization having to secure a single VPN gateway server or portal server, the organization instead has to secure each internal workstation that may be accessed through remote desktop access. Because these internal workstations can be accessed from the Internet, either directly or indirectly, they generally need to be secured nearly as rigorously as full-fledged remote access servers, yet such workstations were usually not designed with that degree of security in mind. Applying compensating controls for each workstation to raise its security to an acceptable level often involves a significant amount of time and resources, as well as acquisition of additional security controls. Also, authentication solutions, such as two-factor authentication capabilities may need to be deployed to each internal workstation using remote desktop access.

Generally, remote desktop access solutions should only be used for exceptional cases after a careful analysis of the security risks. The other types of remote access solutions described in this section offer superior security capabilities.

Direct Application Access

Remote access can be accomplished without using remote access software. A teleworker can access an individual application directly, with the application providing its own security (communications encryption, user authentication, etc.). The application client software installed on the telework client device initiates a connection with a server, which is typically located at the organization's perimeter (e.g., in a demilitarized zone [DMZ]).

One of the most common examples of direct application access is Web-based access to email, also known as Webmail. The teleworker runs a Web browser and connects to a Web server that provides email access. The Web server runs HTTP over SSL (HTTPS) to protect the communications, and the Webmail application on the server authenticates the teleworker before granting access to the teleworker's email. For cases, such as Webmail, that use a ubiquitous application client (e.g., a Web browser), direct application access provides a highly flexible remote access solution that can be used from nearly any client device.

For the same reasons discussed earlier, the direct application access architecture is generally only acceptable if the servers being accessed by the teleworkers are located on the organization's network perimeter, and not internal networks. Servers on the perimeter are directly accessible from the Internet, so they should be well-secured to reduce the likelihood of compromise. Many organizations choose to provide direct application access to only a few lower-risk applications that are widely used, such as email, and use tunnel or portal methods to provide access to other applications, particularly those that would be at too much risk if they were directly accessible from the Internet.

Appendix 4. Legal Rights of Teleworkers

As a teleworker, you should be aware of your legal rights. While most teleworkers fall under the category of "regular workers," others may have special needs, i.e., they may be older, disabled, or having issues dealing with elderly relatives/child care, among other things.

Labor Laws for Regular (W2) Workers

Although many laws have been around for decades, with implications still being felt today, some are more recent. These laws affect all regular (W2) workers, regardless of whether they are full-time telecommuters or office personnel. The key words here are "full time."

The federal laws prohibiting job discrimination are:

Title VII of the Civil Rights Act of 1964, which prohibits employment discrimination based on race, color, religion, sex, or national origin.

The Equal Pay Act of 1963 (EPA), which protects men and women who perform substantially equal work in the same establishment from sex-based wage discrimination.

The Age Discrimination in Employment Act of 1967 (ADEA), which protects individuals age 40 or older.

Title I and Title V of the Americans with Disabilities Act of 1990 (ADA), which prohibit employment discrimination against qualified individuals with disabilities in the private sector, and in state and local governments.

Sections 501 and 505 of the Rehabilitation Act of 1973, which prohibit discrimination against qualified individuals with disabilities who work in the federal government.

The Civil Rights Act of 1991, which, among other things, provides monetary damages in cases of intentional employment discrimination.

The U.S. Equal Employment Opportunity Commission (EEOC) enforces all of these laws. EEOC also provides oversight and coordination of all federal equal employment opportunity regulations, practices, and policies. (Source: http://www.eeoc.gov/abouteeo/overview_laws.html)

Another federal law, the Family and Medical Leave Act of 1993 (FMLA) allows for up to 12 work weeks of unpaid leave during any 12-month period for eligible employees to care for a newborn child, seriously ill family members, or if they themselves develop a serious health condition, among other contingencies. (Source: http://www.dol.gov/esa/whd/fmla)

Each state has also its own laws against discrimination in addition to enforcement agencies. And although there are few laws preventing discrimination regarding sexual orientation (gays, transgender), managers should be sensitive to this area, as well. Given the recent controversy about same-sex marriage, it only follows that the rights of gays will be eventually addressed in the workplace. The cold reality is that many of these issues, particularly relating to age and sex, do come into play in decisions regarding hiring and promotion more often than they should.

To protect themselves legally, managers should avoid knowing the employee's age, sexual orientation or even family situation. Although this may seem somewhat stringent, consider the fact that upon legal review, you as manager may be perceived as having utilized this information to make decisions on which employee to promote, terminate, and so forth. Information about equal labor laws can be found at www.eeoc.gov; most states also have a specific Web site for their laws. (Source: Management Basics, Sandra Gurvis)

Additionally, the Fair Labor Standards Act (FLSA) establishes minimum wage, overtime pay, recordkeeping, and child labor standards affecting full-time and part-time workers in the private sector and in federal, state, and local governments. Covered nonexempt workers are entitled to a minimum wage of not less than $7.25 per hour effective July 24, 2009. Overtime pay at a rate of not less than one and one-half times their regular rates of pay is required after 40 hours of work in a work week. The FLSA applies to telecommuters as well; for example, you must pay time-and-a-half to nonexempt employees who work overtime, whether they are home or office-based.

Appendix 5. Safety and Working from Home

When working from home, teleworkers must address issues of personal safety. This is not relevant to telework centers, where appropriate workstations are provided.

Government employees causing or suffering work-related injuries and/or damages at the alternative work site (home, telework center, or other location) are covered by the Military Personnel and Civilian Employees Claims Act, the Federal Tort Claims Act, or the Federal Employees' Compensation Act (workers' compensation), as appropriate. If you are working for a corporation, make sure you know what insurance cover you have. If you are self-employed take out the appropriate insurance.

Appendix

Teleworker Safety Responsibilities (for home-based telework)

- ☐ Provide appropriate telework space, with ergonomically correct chair, desk, and computer equipment.
- ☐ Complete safety checklist certifying the space as free from hazards. This checklist is not legally binding, but details management expectations and, if signed, assumes compliance.
- ☐ Immediately report any work-related accident occurring at the telework site and provide the supervisor with all medical documentation related to the accident. An agency representative may need to access the home office to investigate the accident.

Lighting
Good lighting in your home office is important to reduce eyestrain. Here are some lighting suggestions:
- Make sure lighting isn't too bright.
- Avoid white reflective furniture.
- If you are using a desk lamp, choose a low wattage light bulb. Direct the light toward papers, not eyes.
- Use blinds or drapes to eliminate outdoor light.
- Avoid bright lighting on your monitor.

Monitor
- Adjust the monitor so that the screen is slightly below eye level.
- Position the monitor to minimize glare.
- Clean the screen on a regular basis.
- Position yourself about 20"-24" away from the monitor.
- Center your monitor on the user.
- Keep your head at a comfortable level.

Safety hazards

Whether you work from a home or in an office, work spaces are often full of dangers that threaten the physical well-being of all who enter. Company coworkers or, at home, family members and pets can unknowingly be in harm's way. While some threats are fairly obvious, others can lurk in the most unexpected places.

Office cables and wires are far more than an unsightly nuisance. Slips, trips and falls constitute the majority of general industry accidents. They cause 15 percent of all accidental, job-related deaths and are second only to motor vehicles as a cause of fatalities, according to the Occupational Safety and Health Administration (OSHA). Therefore, keep power adaptors, modems, power strips, hubs, and so on, off the floor. Don't overload electrical outlets and always have a fire extinguisher on hand. Check it at regular intervals to ensure it is still functional. Also make sure filing cabinets and tall bookcases are anchored to the wall, so they can't topple over.

More than five million Americans or 3.8 percent of our population work from home. Whether it's telecommuting or starting a home-based business, Americans are spending more time in home offices that are not ergonomically equipped. The result is more back and neck pain from poorly designed chairs and workspaces and more headaches and eye strain from bad lighting.

"Most people don't give one thought to the chair they are sitting in while they work, yet they will spend years of their lives molded to that piece of furniture," said Mark McLaughlin, MD, of Princeton Brain and Spine Care. "A well-balanced, ergonomic chair at work is one of the best preventative interventions one can do for the spine. It could prevent many episodes of back and neck pain flare-ups and, in some settings, even help prevent spine surgery."

Chair

Your chair is the most important piece of furniture in your office. You want to find a comfortable chair that has the following characteristics:

- ☐ Adjustable height
- ☐ Lower, raise, and tilt backwards
- ☐ 16" to 20" off of the floor
- ☐ Lumbar support
- ☐ Good backrest and wide enough to support shoulders
- ☐ Chair's seat should allow 1"-4" of space between edge of chair and your knees
- ☐ Front edge of seat is curved
- ☐ Five wheels
- ☐ Padded armrests that can lower or raise

Before you purchase your chair, make sure to give it a test drive. If possible, move the chair that you like in front of a desk and see how it feels. Adjust the seat so that your feet are flat on the floor. When you do this, the lumbar support should fit into the small of your back. The chair should fit your body and meet the previously stated guidelines. Although a good chair that is already assembled can cost anywhere from $400 - $2,000, you can get a similar model for much less, provided you're willing to take the time to put it together. Most office supply stores will have several models to "test drive" and select from before making a final purchase.

Desk

Before purchasing a desk, evaluate your needs. What is your profession? What equipment will you be using? How much desktop room will you need? Make sure to allow space for computer equipment, telephone, Rolodex, other office supplies, and writing room. You also need room for heavily used items on your desk, or you might have to constantly stretch, twist, and turn to reach

Appendix

things. You can also use height-adjustable large tables which are cost effective. These tables let you move from keyboard to side table without having to hunch your shoulders.

Keyboard and Mouse

Since it is so important to have your wrists at the right height when using input devices, a tray system is important to consider as an option. Choose a system that has the following features:

- ☐ Height adjustable
- ☐ Adjustable angle
- ☐ Allows for upper arm relaxation by right angle position of arms

The keyboard should be 28"-30" off the floor. If your keyboard is too low, you will slump over it, and if it is too high, you will strain your wrists. A good keyboard will not flatten your hands and bend your wrists; keyboards that are split and/or tilt may be better than the traditional flat model.

A wrist pad for the front of your keyboard will also cushion your wrists. A computer mouse can cause the hand to twist into uncomfortable positions, resulting in wrist injuries. Try to use the mouse with a sweeping movement, instead of a quick, twisting motion. Use your mouse as little as possible or purchase a trackball instead. Trackballs allow for programming a lock button, omitting the need to click and drag.

Posture

Although it can be easy to forget about when in the middle of working, take the time to learn how to sit properly, doing the following:

- ☐ Relax shoulders
- ☐ Wrists straight
- ☐ Back in contact with lumbar support of your chair
- ☐ Legs in contact with your seat
- ☐ Feet on the floor
- ☐ Elbows at a right angle when typing
- ☐ Upper arm and elbow close to body
- ☐ Head and neck straight

If you find yourself slumping over, practice good posture while doing a routine activity, such as watching TV or driving a car. Even being aware that you need to sit up straight can help correct posture and avoid a myriad of problems that can result strain on shoulders, neck, and back.

Home Inspection To home inspect or not to home inspects seems a major point of controversy among managers. The following are some pros and cons regarding home inspections.

From the Telework Exchange:

Q: My organization (I'm a fed) just established a telework directive. As part of the process for approving telework from home, the supervisor is required to inspect the home office for compliance with government safety standards. This seems extreme to me. Is it normal to require home office inspections as a pre-condition to telework?

A: No, it is not a typical government policy or practice. According to information found in the federal government's telework Web site (www.telework.gov), "the agency is not required to visit the teleworker's home to inspect it for safety and ergonomics."

In fact, a requirement for supervisors to inspect home offices should be discouraged. Why? Primarily, because your supervisor is unlikely to be a safety specialist with sufficient knowledge of Occupational Safety and Health (OSHA) rules and regulations to make an informed decision about your home office setup.

A formal approval by your supervisor means that your employer has agreed that your home office meets all applicable regulations. This requirement creates greater liability for the organization and could result in supervisors being more reluctant to approve telework requests. After all, how many supervisors would care to be put in this position, in addition to dealing with the logistics involved in carrying out home office inspections?

There is a better alternative. Many organizations use a "Self-Certification" Safety Checklist, which requires the employee to review their home office against listed OSHA standards and certify that it is compliant. This meets the goal of encouraging a focus on safety without creating a liability for managers. Agencies still reserve the right to inspect home offices, with advance notice, if a concern exists about safety or security issues.

(Source: http://www.teleworkexchange.com/teleworker-03-09g.asp)

The Occupational Safety and Health Administration (OSHA) does not have any regulations governing telework in home offices. The agency issued a directive in February 2000 stating that it won't conduct inspections of employees' home offices, won't hold employers liable for employees' home offices, and doesn't expect employers to inspect their employees' home offices. (See OSHA Directive CPL 2-0.125 for more information.)

OSHA conducts inspections of other home-based work sites, such as "home manufacturing operations," only when it receives a complaint or referral that indicates a violation of a safety or health standard that threatens physical harm or that an imminent danger exists, including reports of a work-related fatality. The scope of the inspection in an employee's home will be limited to

Appendix

his work activities. Note, however, that the OSHA directive deems employers responsible for home work sites if there are hazards caused by materials, equipment, or work processes that the employer provides or requires to be used in an employee's home. (Source: http://hrhero.com/hl/articles/2009/09/18/telecommuting-tips-for-managing-employees-who-work-from-home/)

According to the Office of Personnel Management (OPM), agencies should make sure that the telework employee's work site meets acceptable standards. One option is to have employees complete a self-certification safety inspection form. Onsite inspections, with adequate notice to the employee, are another option.

The following is a workspace safety checklist from the Defense Finance and Accounting Service (DFAS) that can be used as a self-certification checklist, or can be completed by the supervisor, team leader, or other designated inspector.

Workstation Inspection/Safety Self-Certification Checklist For Home-Based Telecommuters

PRIVACY ACT STATEMENT AUTHORITY: Public Law 106-346, Section 359, dated October 23, 2000. PRINCIPAL PURPOSE(S): Information on this form will be used to determine the eligibility of an employee to participate in the Defense Finance and Accounting Service (DFAS) Telecommuting Program, and to communicate requirements of the program to the employee. ROUTINE USE(S): Information on this form may be disclosed to DFAS Human Resources officials, the Department of Defense, and Office of Personnel Management. It may also be used for any of the routine uses as published in the OPM/Govt 1 systems notice. DISCLOSURE: Voluntary, however, failure to complete the form may result in ineligibility for program participation.

Name
Office Symbol
Duty station address
Business telephone
Telecommuting coordinator

Alternate duty station address: describe the designated work area at the alternate duty station designated tour of official duty checklist

The following checklist is designed to assess the overall safety of the alternate duty station. This checklist can be used as a self-certification checklist, or can be completed by the supervisor, team leader, or other designated inspector.

I. WORKPLACE ENVIRONMENT		
1. Are temperature, noise, ventilation, and lighting levels adequate for maintaining employee's normal level of job performance?	☐ Yes	☐ No
2. Are all stairs with four (4) or more steps equipped with handrails?	☐ Yes	☐ No
3. Are all circuit breakers and/or fuses in the electrical panel labeled as to intended service?	☐ Yes	☐ No
4. Do circuit breakers clearly indicate if they are in the open or closed position?	☐ Yes	☐ No
5. Is all of the electrical equipment free of recognized hazards that would cause physical harm? (Frayed wires, bare conductors, loose wires, flexible wires running through walls, exposed wires to the ceiling, etc.)	☐ Yes	☐ No
6. Will the building's electrical system permit the grounding of electrical equipment?	☐ Yes	☐ No
7. Are aisles, doorways, and corners free of obstructions to permit visibility and movement?	☐ Yes	☐ No
8. Are file cabinets and storage closets arranged so drawers and doors do not open into walkways?	☐ Yes	☐ No
9. Do chairs have any loose casters (wheels) and are the rungs and legs of chairs sturdy?	☐ Yes	☐ No
10. Are the phone lines, electrical cords, and extension wires secured under a desk or alongside a baseboard?	☐ Yes	☐ No
11. Is the office space neat, clean, and free of excessive amounts of combustibles?	☐ Yes	☐ No
12. Are floor surfaces clean, dry, level, and free of worn or frayed seams?	☐ Yes	☐ No
13. Are carpets well secured to the floor and free of frayed or worn seams?	☐ Yes	☐ No
14. Is there enough light for reading?	☐ Yes	☐ No
II. COMPUTER WORKSTATION		
1. Is the chair comfortable?	☐ Yes	☐ No
2. Does the employee know how to adjust the chair?	☐ Yes	☐ No
3. Is the employee's back adequately supported by a backrest?	☐ Yes	☐ No
4. When seated, are the employee's feet on the floor or a footrest and are the thighs parallel with the floor?	☐ Yes	☐ No
5. Is the employee satisfied with the placement of the screen and keyboard?	☐ Yes	☐ No
6. Is it easy to read the text on the screen?	☐ Yes	☐ No
7. Does the employee need a document holder?	☐ Yes	☐ No
8. Does the employee have enough legroom at the desk?	☐ Yes	☐ No
9. Is the screen free from noticeable glare?	☐ Yes	☐ No
10. Is the top of the screen paralleled with or slightly above a level gaze when the employee is seated?	☐ Yes	☐ No
11. Is there space to rest the arms while not keying?	☐ Yes	☐ No

Appendix

12. When keying, are the forearms parallel with the floor?	☐ Yes	☐ No
13. When using the keyboard, is the employee's wrist posture neutral when keying?	☐ Yes	☐ No
14. When using the mouse, is excessive reach and arm extension avoided?	☐ Yes	☐ No
15. If you answer No to any of these questions, you are required to see the Safety Officer before the Telecommuting Agreement is signed.		
TELECOMMUTER SIGNATURE		DATE (MM/DD/YYYY)

Telecommuter employees must provide their supervisors a signed copy of this form before they begin to telecommute. Supervisors will provide copies of the form to their telecommuting coordinator and safety office.

Home Worksite Safety Checklist

Name:

Organization:

Address:

City/State:

Business Telephone:

Telecommuting Coordinator:

Alternative Work Site Location:

(Describe the designated work area in the alternative work site.)

A. Workplace Environment

1. Are temperature, noise, ventilation, and lighting levels adequate for maintaining your normal level of job performance?   Yes   No

2. Are all stairs with four or more steps equipped with handrails?   Yes   No

3. Are all circuit breakers and/or fuses in the electrical panel labeled as to intended service?
    Yes   No

4. Do circuit breakers clearly indicate if they are in the open or closed position?
    Yes   No

5. Is all electrical equipment free of recognized hazards that would cause physical harm (frayed wires, bare conductors, loose wires, flexible wires running through walls, exposed wires to the ceiling)?
    Yes   No

6. Will the building's electrical system permit the grounding of electrical equipment?
    Yes   No

7. Are aisles, doorways, and corners free of obstructions to permit visibility and movement?
    Yes   No

8. Are file cabinets and storage closets arranged so drawers and doors do not open into walkways?
    Yes   No

Telework: How to Telecommute Successfully

9. Do chairs have any loose casters (wheels), and are the rungs and legs of the chairs sturdy?
   Yes   No
10. Are the phone lines, electrical cords, and extension wires secured under a desk or alongside a baseboard?
Yes   No
11. Is the office space neat, clean, and free of excessive amounts of combustibles?
    Yes   No
12. Are floor surfaces clean, dry, level, and free of worn or frayed seams? Yes [ ] No [ ]
13. Are carpets well secured to the floor and free of frayed or worn seams? Yes [ ] No [ ]
14. Is there enough light for reading?   Yes   No

B. Computer Workstation (if applicable)

15. Is your chair adjustable?   Yes   No
16. Do you know how to adjust your chair?   Yes   No
17. Is your back adequately supported by a backrest?   Yes   No
18. Are your feet on the floor or fully supported by a footrest?   Yes   No
19. Are you satisfied with the placement of your monitor and keyboard? Yes [ ] No [ ]
20. Is it easy to read the text on your screen?   Yes   No
21. Do you need a document holder? Yes   No
22. Do you have enough leg room at your desk? Yes   No
23. Is the screen free from noticeable glare?   Yes   No
24. Is the top of the screen at eye level?   Yes   No
25. Is there space to rest the arms while not keying?   Yes   No
26. When keying, are your forearms close to parallel with the floor? Yes   No
27. Are your wrists fairly straight when keying?   Yes   No

Employee's Signature and Date: _____
Immediate Supervisor's Signature and Date: _____
Approved [   ] Disapproved [   ]
Please return a copy of this form to your telecommuting program coordinator.

* This checklist was developed by the General Services Administration.

Safety issues that must be addressed:

☐ Electrical outlets are grounded.

☐ Cords and plugs have three wires/prongs.

☐ Interconnecting cables are out of the way, tied together, or covered to minimize the danger of tripping over them and reduce amount of dust they hold.

☐ Never allow cords to interfere with machine operation.

☐ Ensure that plugs are locked or securely inserted into the outlets.

Appendix

- ☐ Use surge protector or master switch. Do not overload extension cords or outlets.
- ☐ Periodically inspect all cords and plugs. Repair or replace them immediately when problems are identified.
- ☐ Ensure that cords are behind desks and tables so there is no danger of tripping over them.
- ☐ Ensure that cords do not interfere with machine operation.
- ☐ Ensure that phone is easily accessible in designated office area.
- ☐ Heavy items are on secure stands and are child-proofed.
- ☐ Equipment is placed near the wall and away from walkways and doors to prevent anyone from tripping or bumping into it.
- ☐ Keep liquids away from the equipment.
- ☐ Keep materials filed or on shelves and out of the way. Store heavier materials in bottom drawers of filing cabinets.
- ☐ Desks, tables, and filing cabinets are placed near the walls and away from walkways and doors.
- ☐ Cabinet and desk drawers are closed when not in use.
- ☐ When using your computer, ensure that the desk or table height is approximately 27 to 39 inches from the floor, allowing your forearms to be parallel to the floor and wrists straight. Leave space in front of your keyboard for the heels of your hands to rest while you are keying.
- ☐ Ensure working surfaces are smooth and free of sharp and jagged edges.
- ☐ Inspect desks and tables to ensure that joints and screws are tight.

SMOKE DETECTORS: The employee's alternative work site should be equipped with the appropriate number of smoke detectors that are properly installed and tested periodically to ensure that they work.

STORAGE: The storing of any item on top of tall furniture or cabinets should be avoided. To permit this practice sets the stage for many types of injuries. Employees attempting to place things on top of furniture or cabinets can strain themselves, and can fall if chairs are used in place of ladders or even if ladders are used incorrectly. The items themselves can fall, striking employees. It is best to limit storage to designated storage rooms/areas. Properly arranged, such rooms/areas will have secured shelves, adequate aisles, proper lighting, and will be maintained in a state of good housekeeping.

A good practice is to limit storage height to maintain a minimum of 18 inches clearance from the ceiling in general, and from light fixtures and other electrical equipment in particular. Check to see that heavy items are stored on lower shelves. Have a ladder or approved step stool available so you can safely reach high places within the work or storage area.

OFFICE PRACTICES: Certain office practices can be hazardous. File cabinets can cause accidents in many ways. If located near entrance doors or aisles, drawers left open can become a bump or trip hazard. If the upper drawers are fully utilized while the lower drawers are nearly empty, the cabinet can tip over when the upper drawers are pulled out. A good rule is to never open more than one file drawer at a time. Close it when leaving the file cabinet – even for a brief period.

HEATERS: Care should be exercised when using portable heaters. Be sure that the heating element is guarded against accidental contact, positioned not too closely to furniture or other combustibles, and that a tip-over switch cuts off electrical power to the heating element if the heater is knocked over. This feature could prevent the heater from starting a fire. Kerosene heaters should not be used in the work area.

COFFEE POTS OR SIMILAR ITEMS: Use of coffee pots and similar items should be placed out of normal work areas and on a noncombustible surface. If an electrical short-circuit occurs, quick action is necessary to prevent a fire. Be sure that all of these types of electrical appliances are turned off at the end of the day, or when leaving the alternate work site.

RADIATORS: Some older homes use radiators for heat instead of the more modern forced air systems. If your work area has radiators, be sure not to place combustible or flammable articles on or near them. Also check to ensure that electrical power cords are not allowed to drape across them.

VIDEO DISPLAY TERMINALS: Video Display Terminals (VDTs) are word processors or computer terminals which display information on a screen. Safe use of VDTs can prevent employee injury. Because of the expanding use of VDTs, concerns have been expressed about their potential health effects. Complaints include excessive fatigue, eyestrain and irritation, blurred vision, headaches, stress and neck, back, arm, and muscle pain. Other concerns include physical discomfort, and cumulative trauma disorders.

Visual symptoms can result from improper lighting, glare, distance from the screen, positioning of the screen, or copy material that is difficult to read. VDT operators can reduce eyestrain by temporarily looking away from the VDT, doing eye exercises, switching to other work or adjusting the brightness of the VDT screen.

VDT users are subject to the risk of developing various musculoskeletal and nerve disorders, such as cumulative or repetitive motion disorders. Carpal Tunnel Syndrome (CTS), a cumulative trauma disorder, is caused by repetitive wrist-hand movement and exertion. When irritated, the tendons and their sheaths housed inside the carpal tunnel swell and press against the nearby median

Appendix

nerve. The pressure causes tingling, numbness, or severe pain in the wrist and hand. CTS can be reduced by stopping or limiting VDT activity, by maintaining proper posture, or, as a last resort, surgery.

DESK: The height of the work surface should be comfortable for most uses (computer work, writing, and reading). Conventional desk surfaces are usually 29 inches high, which is adequate for most tasks. The height recommended for a computer surface is 26 inches.

SEATING: The chair is probably the most important piece of furniture in your work area. Experience has shown that a good ergonomically designed swivel chair, properly adjusted to fit the teleworker's height and work surface, will help improve productivity and avoid backache, neck strain, and disabilities, such as CTS. The seat should be adjustable, and the height (which is measured from the floor) of the top surface of the seat should be 15 to 21 inches. The height and angle of the backrest should be adjustable, and it should provide support for the lower back. Armrests should be substantial enough to provide support, but not so large as to be in the way.

LIGHTING: The lighting in your work area can affect comfort, visibility, and performance. Whether you're using natural light or artificial lighting, it should be directed toward the side or behind your line of vision, not in front or above it. Bright light sources can bounce off working surfaces and diminish your sense of contrast.

NOISE: Depending on your preferences, noisy or totally noise-free environments can be distracting and stressful. Some background sound, such as music, can be beneficial for maintaining a level of productivity and reducing boredom.

Appendix 6. Samples of Teleworking Policies

This section contains a number of teleworking policies and agreements which give an idea of the scope and depth that they cover. You could be asked to sign a document similar to one of these.

Example 1.

[Organization name] has established a pilot program to examine how teleworking can contribute to organizational objectives and employee well-being. This policy provides guidance for teleworkers, employees not teleworking, and management.

Purpose

Teleworking is defined by [NAME] as the practice of working at home for a limited number of days instead of working at the [NAME] office. Telework is a work alternative that [NAME] offers to some employees when it would benefit both [NAME], and the employee. Teleworking is not a formal employee benefit, but a work-scheduling practice that helps employees balance the demands of their work and personal lives. Teleworking is an earned privilege, not a universal benefit or employee right.

An employee's compensation, benefits, work status, and work responsibilities will not change due to participation in the telework program. Telework employees must comply with all organizational rules, policies and procedures.

Eligibility

Candidates for telework must be employees of [NAME] with a history of satisfactory or better performance ratings. The opportunity to telework must be approved by an employee's supervisor, who is ultimately responsible for the decision to continue or discontinue teleworking by the employee, following appropriate notification to the teleworker.

Selection of employees to participate in the Teleworking Pilot Program shall be based on specific, written, work-related criteria including:

- ☐ Employee responsibilities
- ☐ Need for, and nature of, interaction with other staff and external clients
- ☐ Need for use of specialized equipment
- ☐ Availability of other qualified employees onsite
- ☐ Employee job performance

Employees that are considered for teleworking must be able to work independently, be a self-starter, and demonstrate attention to work time and productivity. An employee must have a satisfactory or better performance level with no record of performance or conduct issues. The resources that an employee needs to do his/her job must be easily transportable or available electronically.

The decision to allow an employee to telework will be made by the employee's supervisor in consultation with Human Resources. Eligibility and suitability of employees to participate in teleworking will vary around departments and business units, depending on the function and responsibilities of the employee. Each department must maintain some minimum complement of employees who work onsite at the [NAME] office in order to function effectively.

Teleworking is not an alternative to child or elder care and, when applicable, the teleworker must make appropriate arrangements for dependent care, unless there are extreme exceptions approved by management.

Schedule and Hours

Telework hours and overtime hours may differ from regular office work hours, and must be specified in writing, and agreed upon by the supervisor and teleworker. A regular teleworking

Appendix

schedule, including specific days and hours, must be established. Generally, a teleworker will spend one to two days working from home with the remainder of the scheduled hours working in his/her office, on [NAME] premises. The amount of time the teleworker is expected to work per day or per pay period will not change due to participation in the teleworking program.

Deviations from the agreed-upon schedule should be approved in advance by the supervisor. [NAME]'s policy will be followed for all absences.

Supervisors retain the right to require a teleworker to return to the [NAME] office on a regularly scheduled teleworking day, should work situations warrant such an action. This situation is expected to be only an occasional occurrence. If a teleworker is required to return to [NAME]'s office during regularly scheduled teleworking days frequently, the supervisor may re-evaluate the compatibility of the teleworker's position and job responsibilities with respect to teleworking or the specific teleworking schedule.

Teleworkers are required to account for all time worked in accordance with [COMPANY NAME]'s timekeeping policies. It is the teleworker's responsibility to submit an accurate accounting of hours worked in a timely manner. If a teleworker is sick while working at home, or uses other time off, the teleworker must report hours actually worked on his/her timesheet and use composite leave for the remainder of the hours.

Workspace

Teleworkers must have an appropriate work area in their home that considers ergonomics, equipment, adequate workspace, noise and potential disruptions. The teleworker's offsite workspace should provide an adequate work area, lighting, telephone service, power, and temperature control. Additional requirements may vary, depending on the nature of the work and the equipment needed to perform the work.

[NAME]'s liability for job-related accidents will continue to exist during the approved work schedule and in the teleworker's designated work location since the teleworker's home workspace is an extension of [NAME]'s workspace. The teleworker must agree to follow common safety practices and provide a work area for the employee and others who enter it. The designated work location must meet OSHA safety rules for the workplace including: smoke detector; working fire extinguisher; clear, unobstructed exits; removal of hazards that could cause falls; adequate electrical security, and appropriate furniture. If an at-home injury occurs, the teleworker must notify his/her supervisor immediately and follow [NAME]'s policy for on-the-job injury.

Homeowner's insurance and any changes in rates or coverage are the responsibility of the employee. Any increase in the teleworker's home utility costs (excluding increased telephone costs) is the responsibility of the employee.

Federal and state statutory abstracts will be posted at the teleworker's [NAME] office location in lieu of posting them in the employee's home office. Teleworkers should review these notices while on [NAME]'s premises.

Teleworkers should consult their attorney, tax advisor or accountant regarding any legal or tax implications attendant to working at their home or alternative site.

Equipment and Supplies

Office supplies will be provided by [NAME] and should be obtained during the teleworker's in-office work period. Out-of-pocket expenses for supplies normally available in the office will not be reimbursed. Teleworkers are responsible for all supplies, equipment, and/or materials provided by [NAME]. All items remain property of [NAME] and may not be used for personal or other [NAME] use.

[NAME] will reimburse teleworkers for other business-related expenses that are reasonably incurred in accordance with job responsibilities and approved by the supervisor in accordance with [NAME]'s regular policies. Appropriate documentation is required if such expenses are submitted for reimbursement. [NAME] required equipment is listed under JOB REQUIREMENTS.

[NAME] does not assume liability for loss, damage or wear of employee-owned equipment unless otherwise agreed to in writing prior to the occurrence. Maintenance, repair and replacement of [NAME]-owned equipment issued to teleworkers are the responsibility of [NAME]. In the event of equipment damage or malfunction, the teleworker must notify his or her supervisor immediately. [NAME] reserves the right to enter the home work area for inspection of the equipment, if necessary. Repairs to employee owned equipment is the responsibility of the teleworker. In either situation, the teleworker may be asked to report to the office until the equipment is usable.

Teleworkers must take appropriate action to protect company-provided equipment from damage or theft.

[NAME] equipment must be returned to [NAME] when an employee terminates or discontinues the teleworking arrangement.

Teleworkers may use their own equipment (e.g., fax machine, printer, photocopier) provided that no cost is incurred by [NAME]. Repair and maintenance of employee-owned equipment is the responsibility of the teleworker.

Employee Access and Availability

Teleworkers must be available by telephone and email during scheduled hours, with the exception of their scheduled lunch period.

Appendix

If it has been determined that you cannot be connected to the [NAME]'s telephone system and/or computer system, call your supervisor. You may need to return to [NAME]'s office. If you do not follow this procedure, you will not be compensated for time lost for these disruptions.

Security

It is the responsibility of the teleworker to take all precautions necessary to secure proprietary information and to prevent unauthorized access. The teleworker is required to observe all office security practices when working outside [NAME]'s office to ensure the integrity and confidentiality of proprietary information. Steps to ensure the protection of proprietary information include, but are not limited to, use of locked file cabinets, disk boxes and desks; regular password maintenance; firewall; and any other steps appropriate for the job and the environment.

Teleworkers agree to allow an authorized [NAME] representative access to the home work area during pre-arranged times for business purposes as deemed necessary by the supervisor, including safety inspections, equipment installations and repairs, security assurance, retrieval of [NAME]'s property and performance evaluations. To ensure hardware and software security, all software used for teleworking must be approved by the IT supervisor prior to installation and only approved bulletin board systems may be contacted. All software used for teleworking must be virus inspected and each PC must have virus protection software installed.

[NAME] owned software may not be duplicated unless authorized through the license agreement. Restricted access materials shall not be taken out of the office or accessed through the computer unless approved in advance by the IT supervisor.

Liability

It is the responsibility of the teleworker to maintain a safe, professional work site at home that is free from potential safety problems. Teleworkers must certify that their home is free from workplace hazards by completing a safety checklist.

In the case of an injury while working at home, teleworkers must immediately (or as soon as circumstances permit) report the injury to his/her supervisor or the Human Resources Department and request instructions for obtaining medical treatment.

Application Process

Employees wishing to telework will complete a Telework Selection Survey and provide information concerning job responsibilities, proposed teleworking schedule, types of work tasks and activities to be performed at the offsite workspace, description of the offsite workspace and the equipment required. A decision will be made by [NAME] management to select employees for teleworking.

Teleworkers will be required to sign a Teleworking Agreement and complete associated documentation.

Teleworking arrangements will be on a trial basis for their first three months and may be discontinued at any time, at the request of either the teleworker or [NAME]. If a teleworking arrangement is discontinued by [NAME], every effort will be made to provide two weeks advance notice to the employee. However, there may be instances where no notice is possible. Likewise, if an employee elects to discontinue a telework arrangement, the employee should provide notice to his/her supervisor.

Employees that are teleworking at the time this policy is adopted will be permitted to continue teleworking. Existing teleworkers will need to sign the Teleworking Agreement and complete the associated documentation that is required of all teleworkers.

- ☐ **Income Tax.** It will be the teleworker's responsibility to determine any income tax implications of maintaining a home office area. The company will not provide tax guidance nor will the company assume any additional tax liabilities. Employees are encouraged to consult with a qualified tax professional to discuss income tax implications.
- ☐ **Evaluation.** Teleworkers will participate in all studies, inquiries, reports and analyses relating to this program.

Example 2. Sample Telework Suitability Worksheet

1. Do you have quiet space in your house where you can work free of interruptions?

    Yes____   No____

2. Do you feel there is a time of day when you are most productive?

    Yes____   No____

    If yes, what time of day is it? _____

3. How comfortable do you feel working on your own?

    _____ Very comfortable

    _____ Comfortable

    _____ Somewhat comfortable

    _____ Not at all comfortable

    _____ Uneasy

Appendix

4. Check below if you are more comfortable:

_____ Meeting with people to solve problems

_____ Solving problems on your own

5. Does your job require you to meet with other people often?

Yes____   No____

6. When do you feel you work best?

_____ In spurts of activity

_____ By pacing yourself

7. Do you have a lot of short notice, turnaround assignments?

Yes____   No____

8. Which do you prefer?

_____ Concentrating intently on a project until it is done

_____ Taking the project a little at a time with breaks in between

9. Do your job activities allow you to create milestones and other measurable criteria of completion?

Yes____   No____

10. How much do you feel you need the support that a traditional office environment provides?

_____ Definitely don't need it

_____ Like it, but don't need it

_____ Would prefer to have it

_____ Need it to be effective

_____ Cannot work without it

11. How likely are you to be a workaholic?

_____ Very likely   _____ Not very likely

12. Do you consider yourself a well-organized work planner?

Yes____   No____

13. When planning your work schedule, which do you prefer?

_____ Consulting with someone else

_____ Doing it on your own

14. Are you part of a work team?

Yes____   No____

15. Does your office have regular staff meetings?

Yes____   No____

16. Do you and your manager communicate via email on a regular basis?

Yes____   No____

17. Do you meet deadlines for the completion of your work?

_____ Always

_____ Sometimes

_____ Frequently

_____ Almost never

_____ Usually

Example 3. Sample Telework Agreement – Oregon Office of Energy

Telework as a work option for employees can help stem the growth in auto travel and thereby conserve energy, relieve congestion, and improve air quality. The (Organization Name) endorses telework and strives to be an example of how telework can be a successful strategy in developing a more versatile transportation system that is less harmful to (fill in state)'s quality of life. Telework is also consistent with sound business practices and will help the organization be more competitive in attracting talented and skilled employees. Telework can also increase productivity and morale of employees, boost efficiency in the use of space, and reduce operating costs.

Applicability: This policy applies to all employees of (Organization Name).

Policy: It is the policy of (Organization Name) to allow employees to telework when opportunities exist for improved employee performance, reduced commuting miles or organization

Appendix

savings, and meeting customer needs. Telework, also known as telecommuting, may not be suitable for all employees and/or positions. Telework shall be voluntary unless specifically stated as a condition of employment. Telework is not an employee right. This policy creates no employee rights in relation to telework. Management decisions regarding telework are not subject to appeal except as outlined in this policy. Either the (Organization Name) or the employee may discontinue the arrangement at any time, giving two weeks' notice, unless otherwise provided in the Telework Agreement. Telework may be temporarily suspended due to operational needs of the unit. (Organization Name) is committed to improving the capacity for telework by increasing network access from remote locations. However, current system capabilities do not guarantee access to the central work site's computer system. This policy addresses regular telework and medical telework arrangements. This policy does not set conditions for employees whose official workstation is in the home or who may wish to arrange to do work at home on an occasional basis. Arrangements for full-time home-stationed workers shall be arranged on a case-by-case basis.

General Requirements:

1. Employees may apply to telework after completing trial service. Exceptions may be approved by the (Organization Name)'s administrator or designee.

2. Consideration will be given to employees who have demonstrated work habits and performance well-suited to successful telework in cases when the telework provides opportunity for improved employee performance or employee retention, reduced commuting miles, or organization savings. The following guidelines need to be considered:

- ☐ Work habits: Teleworkers must have demonstrated self-motivation, self-discipline, the ability to work independently, the ability to manage distractions, and the ability to meet deadlines.
- ☐ Position: The teleworker's position must have minimum requirements for direct supervision or contact with customers; the teleworker's need for specialized material must be minimal or flexible; and the teleworker's work objectives and tasks must be clearly defined with measurable results.
- ☐ The telework must be arranged so that there is no difference in the level of service provided to the customer and the location of the workplace is not noticeable to the customer.
- ☐ The location of work must not significantly alter the teleworker's job content or the job content of coworkers.
- ☐ The cost of supporting the teleworker (See Supplies, Equipment, Furniture section) must be reasonable in comparison to amount of commuting miles saved.
- ☐ The teleworker's equipment and software must meet organization standards or the central work site can supply an available loaner laptop.
- ☐ The teleworker's needs for Information Services' (IS) support must be minimal.

3. Telework sites must be in Oregon. (Note: This is a current State of Oregon requirement because of workers' compensation and tort liability issues. Please check with your organization's legal and worker's compensation advisors to determine if this issue is relevant to your policy.)

4. In case of injury, theft, loss, or tort liability related to telework, the teleworker must allow agents of the organization to investigate and/or inspect the telework site. Reasonable notice of inspection and/or investigation will be given to the teleworker.

5. Where telework sites are located in the home, the teleworker is responsible for establishing and maintaining the work site.

6. Employees shall sign and abide by the Telework Agreement between the teleworker and the (Organization Name)'s Administrator or designee.

7. The Telework Agreement will be reviewed by the employee supervisor and teleworker during performance review and revised as necessary.

8. Employee supervisors and prospective teleworkers are expected to take training on telework offered by (Organization's name).

Terms of Employment

1. The teleworker's conditions of employment shall remain the same as for non-telework employees. Employee salary, benefits and employer-sponsored insurance coverage shall not change as a result of telework.

2. (Organization Name) policies, rules and practices shall apply at the telework site, including those governing communicating internally and with the public, employee rights and responsibilities, facilities and equipment management, financial management, information resource management, purchasing of property and services, and safety. Failure to follow policy, rules and procedures may result in termination of the telework arrangement and/or disciplinary action.

The teleworker will not be paid for time involved in travel between the telework site and central work site. Travel between the telework site and the central work site will not be reimbursed.

Work Schedule and Accessibility

1. The number of hours worked will not change because of telework. A consistent schedule of telework work days and hours is desirable for many jobs to ensure regular and predictable contact with (Organization Name) staff and others. For some positions, more flexibility in work hours and days is feasible.

2. The Telework Agreement will specify work schedules that are in compliance with Federal Labor Standards Act (FLSA) regulations, (Organization Name) Policy # (fill in).

Appendix

3. The teleworker must get the employee supervisor's advance written approval for working overtime.

4. The telework schedule needs to allow adequate time at the central work site for meetings, access to facilities and supplies and communication with other employees and customers. Telework must not adversely affect customer service delivery, employee productivity, or the progress of an individual or team assignment.

In approving the telework schedule, the employee supervisor will take into consideration the overall impact of the teleworker's total time out of the central work site. Considerations include flex time and compressed work week schedules, meetings, consultations, presentations and conferences. Consideration will also be given to the overall effect of the teleworker's and coworkers' schedules in maintaining adequate communication.

5. The teleworker will attend job-related meetings, training sessions, and conferences, as requested by the employee supervisor. In addition, the teleworker may be requested to attend "short notice" meetings. The employee supervisor will use telephone conference calling whenever possible as an alternative to requesting attendance at short notice meetings.

6. While teleworking, the teleworker must be reachable via telephone, fax, pager, or email during agreed-upon work hours or specific core hours of accessibility. The employee supervisor and teleworker will agree on how to handle telephone messages, including the feasibility of call forwarding, frequency of checking telephone messages, and the need for having a home phone answering machine. Only the teleworker and the teleworker's supervisor will designate what persons will be given the teleworker's home office phone number.

7. The employee supervisor and teleworker will use the most efficient and effective way of handling long distance calls whether that is the use of an organization calling card or reimbursement for long distance business calls. If reimbursement is approved, the teleworker will submit an expense reimbursement request with a log of long distance business calls and a copy of the phone bill to the employee supervisor on a monthly basis.

8. If the central work site is closed due to an emergency or inclement weather, the employee supervisor will contact the teleworker. The teleworker may continue to work at the telework site. If there is an emergency at the telework site, such as a power outage, the teleworker will notify the employee supervisor as soon as possible. The teleworker may be assigned to the central work site or an alternate work site.

Dependent Care

Teleworkers will not act as primary caregivers for dependents during the agreed-upon work hours. This does not mean dependents will be absent from the home during the telework hours.

It means that they will not require the teleworker's attention during work hours. Teleworkers must make dependent care arrangements to permit concentration on work assignments.

Performance Evaluations

The method of monitoring and evaluating performance will rely more heavily on teleworker work results than direct observation.

Telework Site

1. The teleworker will maintain a designated work space that is clean, safe, and free from distractions.

2. In the event of a job-related incident or accident during telework hours, the teleworker needs to immediately report the event to the employee supervisor. The organization does not assume responsibility for injury to any persons other than the teleworker at the telework site.

3. The teleworker will not hold business meetings with clients or customers, the public or professional colleagues at his or her residence. Meetings with other (Organization Name) staff will not be scheduled on a regular basis at the teleworker's residence and must be approved in advance by the employee supervisor.

4. Teleworkers are advised to consult with their insurance agent and a tax consultant for information regarding home work sites. Individual tax implications, auto and homeowners insurance, and incidental residential utility costs are the responsibility of the teleworker.

Supplies, Equipment and Furniture

1. The Telework Agreement must specify all reimbursable costs. Any additional costs related to telework must be authorized by the (Organization Name) Administrator or designee prior to purchase or installation. (Organization Name) will provide standard office supplies (pens, paper, pencils, etc.). Out-of-pocket expenses for supplies normally available at the central work site will not be reimbursed. Teleworkers need to get supplies while at the central work site.

2. Teleworkers shall be responsible for providing home telework site furniture and equipment. Unless approved by the (Organization Name) Administrator and specified in the Telework Agreement, the teleworker will provide his or her own computer hardware and software and whatever data communications and services are needed to complete specified telework tasks. In certain cases, other arrangements may be negotiated between the (Organization Name) Administrator or designee and the teleworker, and documented in the Telework Agreement.

3. The following conditions shall apply to use of supplies, organization records, computers and other organization-owned equipment:

Appendix

- ☐ Use of organization equipment in the home shall be the same as at the central work site.
- ☐ Restricted-access materials shall not be taken out of the central work site or accessed through the computer unless approved in advance by the supervisor.
- ☐ Products, documents, and records used and/or developed while teleworking shall remain the property of the organization, and are subject to organization policies regarding confidentiality and records retention requirements.
- ☐ Products, documents and records that are used, developed, or revised while teleworking must be copied or restored to the (Organization Name)'s computerized records. Records and files temporarily stored on the teleworker's personal computer need to be stored in a way that will allow (Organization Name) easy access, while protecting the teleworker's personal files. It is suggested that all telework-related information be located on a directory designated for telework and that this information be backed up on a disk or on the LAN server.
- ☐ For telework jobs that have security and/or confidentiality requirements, procedures must be established to guarantee protection of confidential information. Procedures may include a locked or secure workplace, computer access passwords, or restricted use of files at the telework site. If security and/or confidentiality issues exist, they need to be addressed in the Telework Agreement.

4. Teleworkers shall be in compliance with all (Organization Name) guidelines for uses of computer hardware and software, including:

- ☐ Need for (Organization Name) standard virus and surge protection on home computers
- ☐ Software licensing provisions
- ☐ Duplication of organization-owned or licensed software
- ☐ Maintaining system security
- ☐ Access to files
- ☐ Passwords

5. (Organization Name) is not responsible for loss, damage, or wear of teleworker-owned equipment. The organization may pursue recovery from the teleworker for organization property that is deliberately, or through negligence, damaged, destroyed, or lost while in the teleworker's care, custody, or control. (Organization Name) is responsible for the deductible on organization property. Repair and/or replacement costs and liability for privately owned equipment and furniture used during telework is the responsibility of the teleworker.

6. Repair and/or replacement costs and liability for organization-owned equipment used during telework is the responsibility of (Organization Name). (Normal use and wear is not as a result of negligence or deliberate damage, destruction, or loss.)

7. The (Organization Name)'s Fiscal and Information Services (IS) sections shall maintain a central inventory of (Organization Name) equipment and software located in the home offices of teleworkers. All (Organization Name) equipment and software used at the telework site must be noted on the Telework Agreement.

Procedure:

To Apply

Employee:

Review Oregon Office of Energy Training Kit "Telework Basics" brochure and Teleworker Self-Assessment; Complete Telework Application and Telework Office Checklist; Submit to employee supervisor or (Organization Name)'s Administrator or Designee.

Employee Supervisor:

Review Oregon Office of Energy Manager's Telework Kit (Manager's video and "Manager's Quick and Easy Guide to Telework") and Teleworker Self-Assessment; Review the Telework Application and Telework Office Checklist; Determine if Telework Application meets general requirements for telework and that work schedule, accessibility issues, dependent care, and equipment issues are satisfactorily addressed.

Request a review by IS to determine if proposed Telework Application meets (Organization Name) equipment and software standards and level of IS support needed. Inform (Organization Name)'s Administrator of the request for telework and consult on any issues raised by the request. If telework request is accepted, refer to the Implementing Telework section of this procedure.

Implementing Telework

Employee Supervisor:

Notify telework applicant that the Telework Application has been accepted.

Employee and Employee Supervisor:

Schedule a time to view telework training video in Oregon Office of Energy Telecommuting Training Kit. View video, discuss telework arrangement and complete Telework Agreement.

Employee Supervisor:

Contact IS staff if computer access is needed. Meet with teleworker and coworkers to address how arrangements will work; discuss concerns and problems. Revise Telework Agreement as needed based on this discussion.

Appendix

Employee and Employee Supervisor:

Sign final Telework Agreement. Employee supervisor will forward Telework Agreement to (Organization Name)'s Administrator for approval.

(Organization Name)'s Administrator or Designee:

Discuss Telework Agreement with employee supervisor; Indicate approval or denial on Telework Agreement form; Return Telework Agreement to employee supervisor.

Employee Supervisor:

If Telework Agreement approved by the (Organization Name) Administrator, notify employee. Notify employee's coworkers and others with whom the employee interacts about the telework schedule. Notify (Organization Name)'s receptionist about the telework schedule and how telephone calls to the teleworker are to be handled. If organization-owned equipment is to be used at home telework site, ensure that it is included in Fiscal and IS sections' central inventory listing of telework equipment and that changes are made to (Organization Name) inventory records, if necessary. Send original Telework Application, Telework Office Checklist and Telework Agreement to (Organization Name) personnel contact. Give teleworker a copy of each and keep a copy of each.

(Organization Name)'s Personnel Contact:

File original telework materials in the teleworker's personnel file; Give a copy to the Fiscal section.

Employee and Employee Supervisor:

Respond to information and survey requests from the (Organization Name) and (Organization Name)'s Employee Services.

Telework Denied/Request for Reconsideration

(Organization Name)'s Administrator or Designee and Employee Supervisor:

If decision is made to deny telework, inform employee of decision. Employee may either accept the decision or request reconsideration by the (Organization Name)'s Administrator. Schedule an appointment with the (Organization Name)'s Administrator, designee, or immediate supervisor.

Employee, (Organization Name)'s Administrator and Employer Supervisor

Confer either in person or by telephone to review telework request, reasons for denial. Determine if telework is still not an option or if a telework arrangement can be implemented. (Organization Name)'s Administrator makes the final determination.

Example 4. Sample Corporate Telework Policy and Agreement

Telework programs are designed to help employees work effectively at home. By understanding the following policies governing teleworking, you'll have a greater awareness of your obligations and responsibilities — as well as the employer's — when working from home.

1. Employee salary, benefits, and employer-sponsored insurance coverage will not change as a result of teleworking.

2. More specific conditions relating to the employee's working at home are detailed in the Telecommuting Agreement, which must be filled out by the employee and his/her supervisor, subject to manager's approval.

3. Since the employee's home workspace is an extension of the employer's office workspace, the employer's liability for job-related accidents will continue to exist during the approved work schedule and in the employee's designated work location. To ensure that safe working conditions exist, the employer will retain the right to make onsite inspections at mutually agreed-upon times.

4. Any changes to the above mentioned schedule or workspace must be reviewed and approved by the supervisor and manager in advance.

5. In most instances, the teleworker will provide his/her own equipment. The employer's equipment in the home office may not be used for personal purposes.

6. Employer-owned software shall not be duplicated.

7. To ensure hardware and software security, all software used for teleworking must be approved by the supervisor and manager before installation.

8. Restricted-access materials shall not be taken out of the office or accessed through the computer unless approved in advance by the teleworker's supervisor.

9. Unless otherwise agreed to in writing prior to any loss, damage or wear, the employer does not assume liability for loss, damage or wear of employee-owned equipment.

10. Office supplies will be provided by the employer and should be obtained during the teleworker's in-office work period. Out-of-pocket expenses for supplies normally available in the office will not be reimbursed. The employer will not provide office furniture for the workspace at home.

Appendix

11. Telework is not a substitute for dependent care. When necessary, teleworkers must make arrangements for dependent care during the agreed-upon work hours.

12. All teleworkers and their supervisors will attend a training session and must comply with the employer's telework policies.

13. All teleworkers and their supervisors will participate in studies to evaluate the telework program.

14. Offering the opportunity to work at home is a management option; teleworking is not a universal employee benefit. An employee's participation in the telework program is entirely voluntary. The employee, supervisor, or manager may terminate telework without cause.

15. The teleworker's conditions of employment with the employer remain the same as non-teleworking employees.

16. While teleworking, the employee should be accessible during the agreed-upon hours. Teleworkers must notify the office if they leave their telework location, similar to notifying a receptionist when leaving the traditional work office during the workday.

Example 5. Telework Policy Template

_____ considers telecommuting to be a viable alternative work arrangement in cases where individual, job and supervisor characteristics are best suited to such an arrangement. Telecommuting allows an employee to work at home, on the road, or in a satellite location for all or part of their regular work week. Telecommuting is a voluntary work alternative that may be appropriate for some employees and some jobs. It is not an entitlement; it is not a company-wide benefit; and it in no way changes the terms and conditions of employment with _____ .

Procedure:

1. Either an employee or a supervisor can suggest telecommuting as a possible work arrangement.

2. Telecommuting can be informal, such as working from home for a short-term project or on the road during business travel, or formal, as will be described in this document. Other informal, short-term arrangements may be made for employees on family or medical leave, to the extent practical for the employee and the organization, and with the consent of the employee's health care provider, if appropriate. All informal telecommuting arrangements are made on a case by case basis, focusing on the business needs of the organization first. Such informal arrangements are not the focus of this policy.

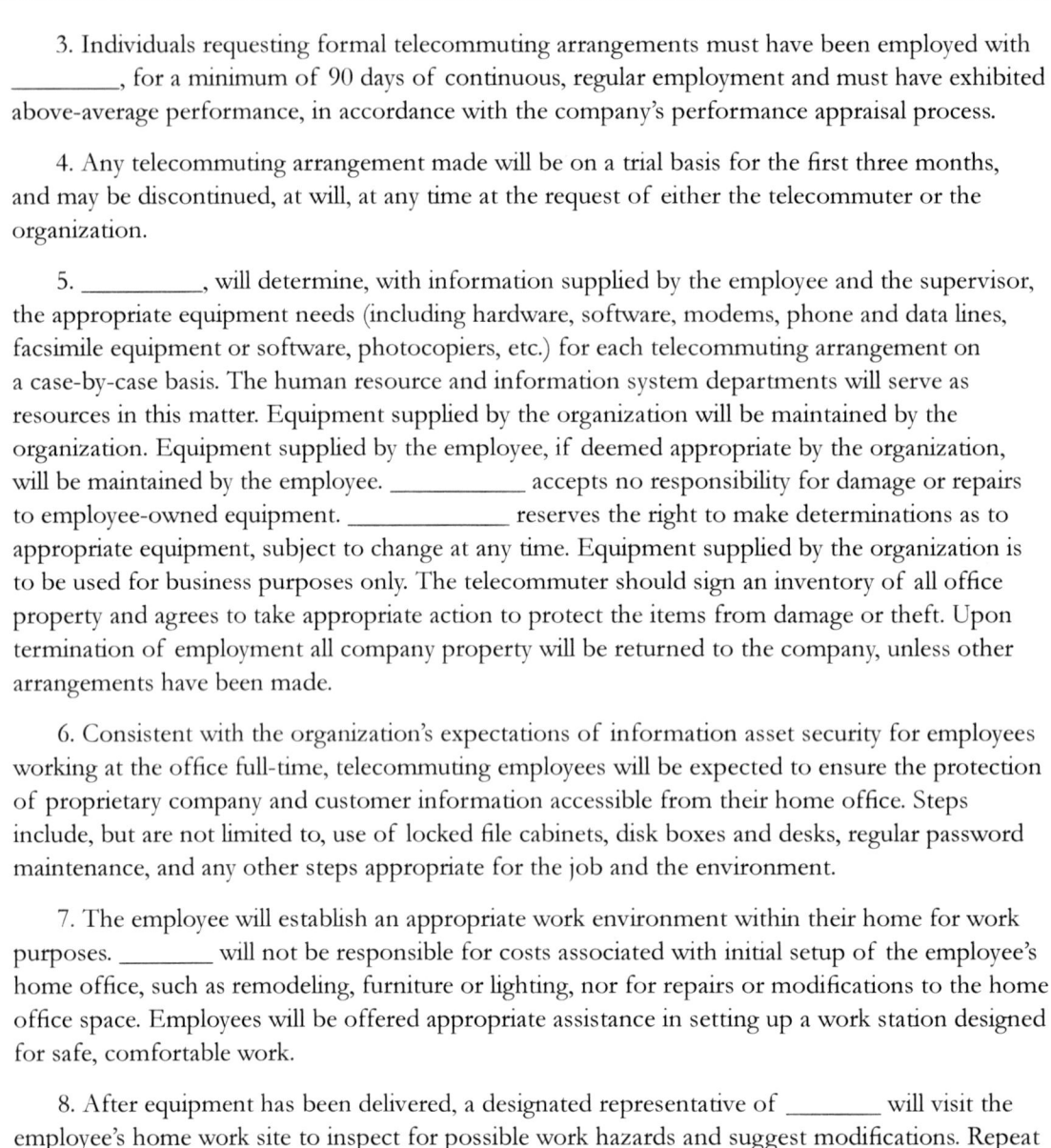

3. Individuals requesting formal telecommuting arrangements must have been employed with _____, for a minimum of 90 days of continuous, regular employment and must have exhibited above-average performance, in accordance with the company's performance appraisal process.

4. Any telecommuting arrangement made will be on a trial basis for the first three months, and may be discontinued, at will, at any time at the request of either the telecommuter or the organization.

5. _____, will determine, with information supplied by the employee and the supervisor, the appropriate equipment needs (including hardware, software, modems, phone and data lines, facsimile equipment or software, photocopiers, etc.) for each telecommuting arrangement on a case-by-case basis. The human resource and information system departments will serve as resources in this matter. Equipment supplied by the organization will be maintained by the organization. Equipment supplied by the employee, if deemed appropriate by the organization, will be maintained by the employee. _____ accepts no responsibility for damage or repairs to employee-owned equipment. _____ reserves the right to make determinations as to appropriate equipment, subject to change at any time. Equipment supplied by the organization is to be used for business purposes only. The telecommuter should sign an inventory of all office property and agrees to take appropriate action to protect the items from damage or theft. Upon termination of employment all company property will be returned to the company, unless other arrangements have been made.

6. Consistent with the organization's expectations of information asset security for employees working at the office full-time, telecommuting employees will be expected to ensure the protection of proprietary company and customer information accessible from their home office. Steps include, but are not limited to, use of locked file cabinets, disk boxes and desks, regular password maintenance, and any other steps appropriate for the job and the environment.

7. The employee will establish an appropriate work environment within their home for work purposes. _____ will not be responsible for costs associated with initial setup of the employee's home office, such as remodeling, furniture or lighting, nor for repairs or modifications to the home office space. Employees will be offered appropriate assistance in setting up a work station designed for safe, comfortable work.

8. After equipment has been delivered, a designated representative of _____ will visit the employee's home work site to inspect for possible work hazards and suggest modifications. Repeat inspections will occur on an as-needed basis. Injuries sustained by the employee while at their

Appendix

home work location and in conjunction with their regular work duties are normally covered by the company's workers' compensation policy. Telecommuting employees are responsible for notifying the employer of such injuries in accordance with company worker's compensation procedures. The employee is liable for any injuries sustained by visitors to their work site. Teleworkers who work from home will not host business-related visitors in their home. Visits by coworkers for business reasons must have prior Director/Supervisor level approval. This restriction is intended to protect the employee and limit liability exposure for the employee and the company.

9. _____ will supply the employee with appropriate office supplies (pens, paper, etc.) for successful completion of job responsibilities. The organization will also reimburse the employee for all other business-related expenses, such as phone calls, shipping costs, etc., that are reasonably incurred in accordance with job responsibilities.

10. The employee and manager will agree on the number of days of telecommuting allowed each month (average of eight days per month), the work schedule the employee will customarily maintain, and the manner and frequency of communication. The employee agrees to be accessible by phone or modem within a reasonable time period during the agreed-upon work schedule.

Managers/Supervisors are responsible to ensure that a sufficient onsite presence is maintained by each telecommuter in their section, and by the section as a whole, to ensure effective communication with supervisors and coworkers. Telecommuters are expected to be onsite for scheduled meetings and management all-hands meetings.

11. Telecommuting employees who are not exempt from the overtime requirements of the Fair Labor Standards Act will be required to record all hours worked in a manner designated by the organization. Due to the nature of the work, telecommuting employees will be held to a higher standard of compliance than office-based employees. Hours worked in excess of those specified per day and per work week, in accordance with state and federal requirements will require the advance approval of the supervisor. Failure to comply with this requirement can result in the immediate cessation of the telecommuting agreement.

12. Before entering into any telecommuting agreement, the employee and manager, with the assistance of the human resource department, will evaluate the suitability of such an arrangement paying particular attention to the following areas:

   a. Employee Suitability - the employee and manager will assess the needs and work habits of the employee, compared to traits customarily recognized as appropriate for successful telecommuters.

   b. Job Responsibilities - the employee and manager will discuss the job responsibilities and determine if the job is appropriate for a telecommuting arrangement.

c. Equipment needs, work space design considerations and scheduling issues.

d. Tax and other legal implications for the business use of the employee's home, will be based on IRS, state and local government restrictions. Responsibility for fulfilling all obligations in this area rests solely with the employee.

13. If the employee and manager agree, and the human resource department concurs, a draft telecommuting agreement will be prepared and signed by all parties and a three-month trial period will commence.

14. Evaluation of telecommuter performance during the trial period will include daily interaction by phone and email between the employee and the manager, and weekly face-to-face meetings to discuss work progress and problems. At the conclusion of the trial period, the employee and manager will each complete an evaluation of the arrangement and make recommendations for continuance or modifications. Evaluation of telecommuter performance beyond the trial period will be consistent with that received by employees working at the office in both content and frequency, but will focus on work output and completion of objectives rather than time-based performance.

15. An appropriate level of communication between the telecommuter and supervisor will be agreed to as part of the discussion process and will be more formal during the trial period. After conclusion of the trial period, the manager and telecommuter will communicate at a level consistent with employees working at the office, or in a manner and frequency that seems appropriate for the job and the individuals involved.

16. Telecommuting is not designed to be a replacement for appropriate child or elder care. Although an individual employee's schedule may be modified to accommodate child care needs, the focus of the arrangement must remain on job performance and meeting business demands. Prospective telecommuters are encouraged to discuss expectations of telecommuting with family members prior to entering into a trial period.

17. Employees entering into a telecommuting agreement may be required to forfeit use of a personal office, workstation or parking space in favor of a shared arrangement to maximize organization office and parking space needs.

18. The availability of telecommuting as a flexible work arrangement for employees of _____ can be discontinued at any time at the discretion of the employer. Every effort will be made to provide 30 days' notice of such a change to accommodate commuting, child care and other problems that may arise from such a change. There may be instances, however, where no notice is possible.

Example 6.

Appendix

Telework Agreement   The Telework Agreement is a written agreement between the employee and the supervisor requiring them to adhere to applicable guidelines and policies. The Telework Agreement is NOT an employment contract and may not be construed as such. Each employee and supervisor must sign the Telework Agreement. Signed agreements must then be submitted to the Telework Coordinator for tracking purposes.

Telework Agreement

This TELEWORK AGREEMENT is made by and between

_____

and _____ (hereinafter referred to as "Employee").

Outlined below are the conditions for teleworking agreed upon by the employee and

_____

Employee's Alternate Work Site

Address:

Alternate Phone Number(s):

Fax Number (if applicable):

Employee's Telework Schedule is:

___Fixed (complete schedule below) or ___Flexible (submit schedule, in advance, each week)

Fixed Schedule

Weekday	Office	Alternate worksite	Start	Finish
Mon				
Tue				
Wed				
Thu				
Fri				

Examples of duties to be performed when teleworking

Telework: How to Telecommute Successfully

Employee Acknowledgement

I understand teleworking is voluntary and that my supervisor or I may end this telework agreement at any time. I also understand that this agreement is not a contract for employment.

Furthermore, by signing this telework agreement I acknowledge I have read and will abide by the NSS Telework Policy, including the Telework Guidelines, Home Office Safety Guidelines, and the Home Office Self-Certification Safety Checklist.

Employee's Signature   Date

Supervisor's Review

_____ I have reviewed the employee's Telework Agreement and Home Office Self-Certification Safety Checklist and approve this request.

_____ I have reviewed the employee's Telework Agreement and Home Office Self-Certification Safety Checklist and I am unable to approve this request at this time for the following reason(s):

Supervisor's Signature   Date

Please Return a Copy of this Form to the Telework Coordinator.

CPSIA information can be obtained at www.ICGtesting.com
Printed in the USA
BVOW061516160312

285363BV00005B/7/P